# Selling Your Company

# SELLING YOUR COMPANY

*The Business Owner's Guide to the Process of Selling a Company and Redeeming the Full Value*

TED FOLKERT

iUniverse LLC
Bloomington

**SELLING YOUR COMPANY**
**The Business Owner's Guide to the Process of Selling a Company and Redeeming the Full Value**



*iUniverse books may be ordered through booksellers or by contacting:*

*iUniverse LLC*
*1663 Liberty Drive*
*Bloomington, IN 47403*
*www.iuniverse.com*
*1-800-Authors (1-800-288-4677)*



*ISBN: 978-1-4917-1464-5 (sc)*
*ISBN: 978-1-4917-1466-9 (hc)*
*ISBN: 978-1-4917-1465-2 (e)*

*Library of Congress Control Number: 2013920806*

*Printed in the United States of America.*

*iUniverse rev. date: 12/10/2013*

*To all of the hardworking entrepreneurs who invested their blood, sweat, and tears in their life's dream*

# CONTENTS

# ACKNOWLEDGMENTS

Thanks to the editors and publishers at iUniverse for their guidance in bringing this book to completion and to Pat Hininger for the initial proofing and editing. Many of the ideas and suggestions expressed here would not have been possible without the affiliation for many years with the International Business Brokers Association and Mergers & Acquisition Source through their ongoing training, education, and certification of practitioners in the business of selling businesses.

# INTRODUCTION

I didn't write this book as a textbook on business accounting or the legal transfer of companies, but its intent is to assist you, the owner of a small or midsize business, in understanding the considerations essential in evaluating, marketing, and selling companies in the small to midsize business market.

I can recall starting out as an entry-level entrepreneur with some financial education but without any business training. I was learning the business, the industry, and the management lessons through the trial-and-error method. There was no business plan except to build a business that would provide a living for the family and create some value for the future. There was no thought of focusing on the essential features that create value for a sale of the company in the future.

After owning and operating businesses engaged in transportation, manufacturing, real estate management, and asset management for forty years and simultaneously serving as a business advisor, business broker, and mergers and acquisitions intermediary for twenty years, I am only too aware of the value of understanding the essential qualities that make a company attractive to someone seeking a viable business acquisition.

Many years of experience gain us a perspective that is impossible to realize at the beginning of our entrepreneurship, no matter how much education, advice, and counsel we receive or acquire initially.

If you, a business owner, had the advantage of these lessons gained from learning by experience and if you had a good understanding of the value drivers of business valuation a little earlier in the process, the benefits could be rewarding during the working years of business ownership and the after years, that is, the time to sell or time to move on.

I don't know how many times business owners I've counseled about exiting their companies have told me that, if they had started the business with a plan to sell the company in the future, they would probably have done things differently. It would be great to begin with twenty-twenty foresight instead of ending up with twenty-twenty hindsight. But we start out with a plan or sometimes none at all to earn a living for ourselves and our families and to build something that will continue to provide our livelihood for years to come. And then, a few years or decades later, reality awakens us to the dilemma of how to exit the company and sustain our livelihood without the income, involvement, and identity that the company has provided for us all those years.

So what do we do with our life's enterprise? How do we go about realizing some value from our biggest asset without continuing to manage it forever? More often than not, the thought through the years was to let family members take it over. Of course, at the early stages, we don't realize that, when that time comes, we may not want them to. Or they may not want to or may not be capable of running it. Or we may need the value that it can bring as a means of support going forward. So, more often than not, the decision is to offer the company for sale to a new owner.

We next realize that it isn't as easy as it seems. It seems that, if we could let the word out that it might be possible to acquire the company, we could then merely sit back and watch the offers come in with the only challenge being to select the best offer and owner for our business, that is, the baby we sired, created, mothered, organized, financed, promoted, and engineered into a good, viable business and a profitable, sustainable stream of income.

If it would only work that way, this book would be of less importance. But because it doesn't work that way, we must face the fact that all business owners are faced with, at some point, the decision of how best to exit the company, to exchange the value that was created over many years for cash, future income for retirement, or estate assets for others or to leave and move on for other reasons. These are some of the most important financial decisions that business owners ever encounter and some of the most stressful and perhaps most miscalculated and mishandled.

The sale of privately owned companies is a big business in and of itself in this country. Thousands of real estate agents, business brokers, seminar promoters, advisors, appraisers, representatives, attorneys, accountants, escrow companies, lenders, merger and acquisition intermediaries, and investment bankers are involved in the business of selling businesses.

Millions of small businesses, tens of thousands of midsize businesses, and thousands of larger businesses are in this country. Many change hands every year. These transactions support the practitioners in the industry and fulfill the exit strategies and acquisition strategies for the players, the buyers and sellers.

The procedures and pitfalls discussed and illustrated here will give you some beneficial insight into the decision-making process, the potential of a successful sale, the value you might realize from a sale, the damage that could occur in the process, and the steps involved in a successful transfer of your company to a new owner.

It should be noted that much of the information provided herein is the opinion of the author and may differ from the opinion of others with knowledge and experience in the business of selling businesses. Financial illustrations are presented, not for the purpose of accuracy or recommended procedures, but to indicate how decision-making can be based in various situations.

You may want to keep three words in mind while reading this book: ready, willing, and able. These three words should apply in many of the examples, suggestions, and cautions discussed and illustrated. And above all, a successful and mutually beneficial sale of a company requires a ready, willing, and able buyer and a ready, willing, and able seller.

# CHAPTER 1

## *An Overview: The Basics of Selling a Company*

Most every business owner will eventually need an exit plan. The reasons will vary.

- The owner is tired of doing what he or she is doing and, consequently, not maximizing the potential of the company. Some practitioners in the sale of businesses consider this the most often cited reason for selling.
- The owner has insufficient sources of capital to maintain a healthy cash flow or grow the company, a very common reason for selling.
- The owner lacks capital, expertise, adequate facilities, or technology. These are unfortunate but frequent.
- An industry is declining due to new technology, unpopularity, or obsolescence.
- The owner wishes to pursue other opportunities, an often-cited reason for selling.
- The owner has a physical or mental condition that prevents or deters required involvement in the company.
- The owner wants to retire from business, the reason for selling that typical buyers prefer most.

Every business either changes hands or ceases to exist at some point. The company could be liquidated, sold, merged, turned over to heirs, reorganized as a public company, or just shut down and ceased to exist. All of these are common methods of an owner exiting a privately held company.

It may be easier to attract a rewarding disposition of your business venture if your business has proven to have viability, growth potential, and a sustainable profitability. Businesses that fit this description attract more attention and more capable buyers. But businesses without these favorable achievements are not necessarily worthless and may also have value to a buyer for reasons other than a continuing stream of income. There may be an opportunity available to the owner to reap some reward for founding, nurturing, and operating the business for a period of years even if the profitability has not been the greatest achievement.

The most commonly desired exit strategy is a sale of the company. If executed favorably, this provides a home for the company and a reward for the owner. Successful transfers of ownership obviously do occur quite often in the small business world and work out well for the seller and the buyer. Unfortunately, that is not always the case. Sometimes, they don't work out so well. Sometimes, the new owner cannot retain the customer base. Sometimes, the new owner is not adequately capitalized due to the impact of purchasing the company and providing working capital and servicing purchase financing used to acquire the company. Buyers and sellers both have a tendency to overlook eventualities and overestimate outcomes. In other words, both are sometimes overly optimistic.

The most important fact that exiting business owners should be aware of is that sometimes a company offered for sale sells and sometimes it doesn't. This next sentence may seem surprising.

Usually, it doesn't sell. If you get the true statistics from an agent, broker, or industry expert, you will find that only about 20 percent of businesses listed for sale actually sell. Why is this? The reasons for a company not selling are many.

- Overpricing can make it impossible for a typical buyer to obtain adequate financing or may prevent the buyer from realizing a reasonable return of the investment required to acquire the company.
- Most buyers are not willing to accept unprofitability. Generally, if the current owner is unable to make a profit, it is too big a risk to assume that a new owner could do so.
- Too much of the revenue of the company is concentrated in one or a few customers. The loss of one or more could cause failure.
- The owner's relationship with the customers is such that it may be difficult to maintain the level of revenue after the owner leaves.
- The company may require expanded facilities or a new location to succeed.
- New technology or obsolescence may be causing declines that cannot be resolved.
- The area where the company is located may have deteriorated and be unable to support a sustainable level of revenue.
- Potential buyers may lack adequate equity capital to obtain additional financing of the transaction.
- There may be no source of financing for a particular industry or area.

- Potential buyers may be unable to assure themselves of a continuation of the income stream due to contracts expiring or limited demand.

The most prudent approach to entering the process of selling your company is to get a good understanding of the important elements of a successful transaction and to follow the steps essential in providing an offer of the opportunity that will be successful for the buyer and meets the goals of the seller.

That is what most business buyers want and need. That is what most successful business sellers provide. That is what is essential for a successful sale of a business—one that turns out well for all parties and survives the pitfalls and unconsidered circumstances of the many changes that take place for the seller, buyer, employees, customers, and others directly affected in the outcome.

There are many essential steps to a successful sale of a company. The priorities should be:

1. **Determining the objectives of the seller.** The seller should determine his or her objectives in exiting the company, whether he or she is cashing out, entering into another business, retiring, establishing an income stream for retirement, making tax considerations, or a long list of other considerations.
2. **Determining the value of the company.** Valuation helps determine a realistic range of values that a transaction might bring for the seller. The potential value that can be realized from a sale of the company will help the seller determine if the sale will meet his or her objectives, whatever they may be.

3. **Preparing the company for sale.** Preparing the business for sale can enhance or lessen the perceived value of the company. The value may be there, but the first impression or a more thorough examination may fail to demonstrate the quality of the operation, the diligent management, or the potential of future growth of the company.
4. **Preparing an offering of sale.** Determining the method of offering the business for sale is important. You can offer your company either through representation by someone in the business of selling businesses or as a for-sale-by-owner offering. Both methods have advantages and disadvantages that should be fully understood in the decision-making process.
5. **Preparing a marketing plan.** Preparation of a marketing plan and offering information to attract potential buyers is another important phase of an offering for selling your company. Important in this phase is selection of methods of attracting potential buyers, such as Internet ads, e-mail campaigns, direct mail to potential buyers, newspaper ads, and a listing on businesses-for-sale websites.
6. **Implementing the marketing plan.** Meeting and conferring with respondents, providing facility tours for qualified potential buyers, and providing face-to-face meetings with accounting and legal advisors are all functions of this phase of the process.
7. **Providing necessary information for the sale**. Preparation of comprehensive information about the company is important for presentation to qualified parties who have expressed an interest in an acquisition. Information includes a description of the business operations, financial statements,

current and historical sales records, employee staffing, management staffing, and projection of growth potential.

8. **Negotiating the terms and conditions.** This phase of the sale process includes receiving offers, proposals, or letters of intent to purchase and negotiate an agreement of price and terms. Terms should include assets included or excluded, financing terms, training and transition assistance for buyer, employment agreements, due diligence period, contingencies, closing procedures, and an integration period for acclimation of the buyer with the customers, employees, vendors, and the general operation of the business.
9. **Completing due diligence and documentation.** Documents—including a purchase and sale agreement, a bill of sale, a promissory note, a schedule of assets, an inventory list, a noncompetition agreement, and other documents necessary for opening escrow and closing the transaction—become the important issue.
10. **Integrating the buyer.** Integration of the new owner with employees, customers, vendors, and others involved in the business provides a period of training and transition assistance to fulfill acclimation of the buyer with all aspects of the business and to achieve cooperation of those essential in the successful operation of the company.

I learned about these critical steps during years of business ownership and participating in training sessions, seminars, and professional courses of study required for certification as a Certified Business Intermediary and from the experience provided by participation in many engagements with companies and transactions of business sales. Much of my education has been provided through an affiliation with the International Business Brokers Association, M&A Source, the Association for Strategic Planning, and the Association for Corporate Growth. These organizations and the ongoing training they inspire has provided the basis for many successful years of practice in the business of selling businesses and a thorough understanding of the steps to success and the avoidance of failure in the transfer of ownership of privately owned companies.

# CHAPTER 2

## *First Things First—The Objectives*

Watching a business sale transaction progress through the various steps, from the initial decision of going to market to documentation, and then watching it all fall apart at the last minute, will emphasize the importance of following a thoughtful plan throughout the arduous process. The best way to avoid an unhappy ending of a sale transaction is to take first things first.

### What Should Come First?

What should come first? Finding a buyer? Preparing the necessary documents? Discussing it with your employees, lenders, customers, and vendors? None of these should probably come first. The following should be considered the most important first steps:

Get a good idea of the fair market value of your company, one that you can support to a buyer's satisfaction by demonstrating your previous performance and supporting the likelihood of a continuation of success.

Identify, with certainty, the objectives you wish to achieve if you should realize a successful disposition of your company and determine the cost of or ongoing cost requirement of those objectives.

Determine if the value of your company, if received in a successful transfer of the company, will be sufficient to finance the achievement of your personal objectives.

And the answer is: 1 + 2 = 3.

If the fair market value of your company does not seem likely to fulfill your objectives, then you should either reevaluate your objectives or wait until number one will support number two. If you are unlikely to make this equation work, then you should do nothing until it can. The numbers in the equation can always change, and they often do over time, but they still need to add up, or the deal will probably either fail or turn out badly.

## A Case Study about Verifying Your Objectives

> Two partners with significant backgrounds in the industry founded and operated a food distribution company on the West Coast. This enabled them to build a good client base for their new enterprise over a period of six or seven years. They had a trained staff and good rapport with suppliers, enabling them to acquire exclusive distributorships for some seafood and deli products. They developed a private label line of their own that was adding additional business and enhancing customer loyalty and retention. One of the partners wanted to sell the company in order to take advantage of an opportunity in another country. The other and his wife wanted to go into the deli retail business, a less stressful life with good expansion potential. They expressed these objectives as their decision to offer their company to market. I was engaged to find them a buyer. The process began: evaluation, preparation, advertising,

> inquiries, correspondence, meetings, visits to the facilities, disclosures, offers, and letters of intent. And eventually, about twelve months from the time the initial engagement began, a purchase and sale agreement with a foreign buyer was prepared. The buyer was well experienced in the industry with adequate funding, and he was intent upon finding an opportunity in this country. The partners seemed pleased with the agreed price. The sale process moved forward. Due diligence was completed, and closing of the transaction was in sight. So what happened next? You guessed it. One of the partners sat down with his wife and had a heart-to-heart discussion about the value they would receive from the proceeds, the cost to fund their planned new enterprise, and their future financial obligations. They got cold feet. They backed out, and the deal failed. Both the other partner and the buyer were furious, and the broker was seriously disappointed, but none of that mattered. It takes two to tango, and one wasn't dancing.

This case study exemplifies the importance of determining value, identifying objectives, and making sure in advance that the sale proceeds will fulfill the objectives. If not, what is the point of going forward? As the seller, you have exposed confidentiality of your business operations. You have made your employees aware that you intended to leave the business. You have wasted the time of the professionals who worked the transaction, and you have squandered your own time and focus.

## Questions for You, the Seller, to Consider

Why do you think you want to sell your company? Do you want to open a new business? If so, what are the capital requirements? Will the potential sale proceeds provide the necessary capital? How long will it require for you to become profitable in the new enterprise? Will you have sufficient funds to sustain your lifestyle until such time as your new enterprise is profitable? Do you want to acquire another company? What will the acquisition cost be? What will the other capital requirements be, such as working capital or improvement costs?

Do you plan to retire? That is certainly a good reason and the one most desirable for the typical buyer. The buyer will usually be more at ease and have less anxiety about hidden failures and undisclosed negative aspects of the business. The buyer will usually be less concerned about the seller starting another company later and competing for the customer base.

If you are going to retire, what will your financial requirements be after you do so? Will they be less than they are now? How much income going forward will you require to sustain your lifestyle? Most retirees' financial obligations don't change much after retirement unless they downsize or change their lifestyle.

In order to sustain your lifestyle, how much income must you maintain? Will your retirement benefits cover your financial obligations? Do you have savings or other investments that you can rely on to cover your financial obligations? Or will you need to sell your company for enough to cover the nut?

If you sell your company for $500,000, how long will that money last? If you invest the proceeds, how much will they earn? If you are required to pay income tax on the capital gain from the sale, how much will you have left?

All these questions deserve answers and actually require answers if you are going about the process prudently and proving out the numbers before you get to the closing of the sale. Otherwise, not only could you be guilty of causing everyone lots of wasted time and money, you could be subjecting yourself to legal liability for monetary losses of the parties involved, a forcing of the closing under a demand for specific performance of the contract and fees for legal representation of you and the buyer, and fees for any brokers or advisors who may have been involved. So make sure the deal will work for you before you sign your name to the contract.

In order to make sure the deal will work for you, you must first have decided what your objectives are and determined both the funding required to fulfill your objectives and your company's fair market value. Then you will be ready to do the old 1 + 2 = 3.

# CHAPTER 3

## *Determining the Company's Value*

Valuation of companies has filled lots of books, classrooms, and educational conferences. It is, of course, the element of a sale transaction that can make it happen or fail, so it should be done early in the decision-making process.

### Methods of Valuation

If you read the many books written on the subject, you will find unlimited methods to place a value on a company. Professionals preparing appraisals of companies or intermediaries preparing opinions of value primarily use these methods. It should be helpful for the business owner to have a general understanding of the methods that they may encounter. Although the number of valuation methods could become a lengthy course of study, we will discuss four types of methods and several variations of the method categories to determine the value of a company:

- **Asset-Based Valuation:** the assets the company owns
- **Income-Based Valuation:** the income the company earns
- **Market-Based Valuation:** the sale price comparisons of similar companies

- **Rule-of-Thumb-Based Valuation:** the sale price comparisons of similar companies, which can be based on income, sales, or size factors

Strategies and synergies that may affect the value for certain buyers influence these methodologies. There are variations of these methods used throughout the industry for various types of companies, objectives of the acquirer, and financial structures of the subject company or the acquiring individual or company. Each method has different considerations of the aspects and conditions of the companies and various procedures to determine value. What may have value for one buyer may not have worth for another. It depends upon his or her objectives in acquiring the company.

## Descriptions of Valuation Methods

### Asset-Based Valuations

- **Net asset value method:** This method of determining value uses the market value of the tangible assets and the appraised value of intangible assets. Competent appraisers would determine the fair market value of tangible assets—furniture, fixtures, equipment, inventory, and real estate. Industry-knowledgeable appraisers would determine the value of intangible assets—goodwill, special processes, patents, and copyrights. Any liabilities being transferred to the buyer would be deducted from the value of the assets. This method can be difficult to support. The appraised value of intangible assets can be arguable at best. In order for this method to have substance, mutually agreed-upon appraisers would be imperative.

- **Liquidation value method:** This method bases value on the fair market value of assets sold in an orderly manner over a specified period of time, less all liabilities. This would require a comprehensive valuation or appraisal of assets by qualified industry appraisers and an ample period of time for the orderly sale of the assets.

**Income-Based Valuations**

- **Discounted cash flow method:** The term "cash flow" can vary with different methods of valuation, but it is generally considered the net income of the business without deducting various noncash expenses such as depreciation, amortization, and other nonoperational expenses such as interest, taxes, owner's perquisites, above-market owner salaries, and above-market facility rents paid to the company owner. Depreciation and amortization are noncash deductions. They are usually structured for tax purposes and not generally deducted in calculating cash flow. Interest is a cost of capital, and debt principal reductions are debt repayments. These are not operating expenses, so they are usually not deducted in calculating cash flow. The cash flow of the company for a select number of years is calculated. It is then projected into the future for a select number of years based upon the perceived sustainability of earnings. This calculation is then added to a predetermined termination value at the end of the period of years used in the projection. The value of the future earnings is then discounted to present value for the specified period. The sum of these calculated earnings and the termination value is considered the fair market value of the company. Many practitioners say that this is the standard of the industry for evaluating middle-market- sized companies.

- **Capitalization of earnings method:** A selected definition of earnings of the company such as earnings before interest, taxes, depreciation, and amortization (EBITDA) or some other definition of earnings is multiplied by a specified number of years. The number of years is based upon the perceived sustainability of earnings for the specified period of time and adjusted by various risk factors, such as the anticipated risk of failure or diminished earnings of the company. The projected period of earnings and the risk factors applied would be determined by reviewing and projecting historical earnings and considering industry trends and the financial strength of the subject company.
- **Excess earnings method:** This method identifies an above average rate of return created by intangible assets of a given company. The average rate of return must be determined for the tangible assets by comparison with comparable companies. The excess earnings above the norm would then be attributed to intangible assets of the target company. The capitalized value of tangible assets is added to the capitalized value of intangible assets, such as goodwill, with intangible assets receiving a higher rate of return based on acceptable factors, a method reflecting both subjective factors and the conjecture of the evaluator.
- **Economic profit method:** This method uses the calculation of the net operating income, less the adjusted taxes, less the cost of invested capital for a period of years. A predetermined

termination value is added to the calculation, and the projected future earnings would then be adjusted to present value. The cost of invested capital is determined by the invested capital times the weighted average cost of capital of comparable companies. This is a seldom used method but is sometimes preferred for capital-intensive companies.

## Market-Based Valuations

- **Comparable companies method:** This method uses the comparison of the subject company with other comparable companies in size range, industry, or region with adjustments for variations. This method is quite subjective because no two companies are alike in all respects but are dissimilar in many. Comparisons can be arguable when considering reasonable adjustments for variations.

## Rule-of-Thumb Valuations

- **Rule-of-thumb method:** This method is based on prior sales of similar companies of comparable size and in the same industry. This method is often utilized in valuation of small companies in an industry with an adequate number of similar companies for comparison. It can provide a good comparison and support a multiple-of-earnings valuation. Rules of thumb are sometimes based on multiples of earnings, sales, or other factors in the given industry.

The above summary of valuation methods is a general description of methods, and it is intentionally brief and incomplete and should only be relied upon if used by financial advisors with knowledge and experience in valuation of business enterprises. No matter what method of valuation is used to determine the fair market value of your company, valuation is subjective and based upon judgment factors of the evaluator. As judgments vary between business appraisers and others expressing their opinions of value, the calculated number of any valuation should not be considered cast in stone. Value judgments are always arguable, and no final judge can rule in a sale transaction, except a ready, willing, and able buyer and ready, willing, and able seller.

## Defining What We Are Selling

A good question to ask yourself when you are thinking about the value of your company is, "What am I really selling?" We could come up with lots of answers to that question, such as:

- I'm selling a going venture.
- I'm selling the blood, sweat, and tears I put into this company all those years.
- I'm selling an opportunity for someone to take it from here and build it bigger and more profitable.
- I'm selling something I am proud of and that someone else can be proud of.

These statements could all be true; however, when it comes down to the cold, hard facts and it is time for someone to sign the deal and write the check, you are really selling a future stream of income. What happened in the past, the historical earnings and historical performance of the company, are important facts about the company and a basis for evaluation of past performance, but you can't sell past performance. Those years are gone. All you can sell now is future income. You have to be able to convince the buyer of future income.

## Other Valuation Considerations

- **Valuation is not an exact science.** Historical financial figures speak for themselves, but projecting them into the future is subjective and depends on many assumptions that cannot be stated with certainty. The numbers reflected on financial statements and tax returns are often influenced by tax considerations and may be misleading, so it is important in valuing your company to adjust for such practices and to consider the variables that may apply to a given buyer with a different financial structure and various value drivers.
- **Value may differ for two potential buyers.** Consideration must be given to strategies and synergies. These elements of valuation are sometimes known and sometimes not known by the seller and applied by the buyers in their respective valuations of the acquisition.
- **A buyer is not buying historical earnings.** A buyer is buying some assurance of future earnings and growth potential, which can be supported by historical earnings and could be generated by the potential buyer's promotion or business plan. But in most cases, there must be convincing assurance of future earnings and an adequate return on investment in order to satisfy a buyer's anxiety and fear of failure.

# CHAPTER 4

## *Defining Valuation Terms and Processes*

### Income Valuation Terms and Processes

Most business valuations are based upon income in one form of interpretation or another. It is helpful in understanding the typical conversation of business valuations to define the terms and processes used to arrive at the type of earnings preferred in valuation of various sizes and types of businesses. The most common definitions are as follows:

- **Earnings after taxes (EAT):** For large companies, the often-used definition of earnings is what is referred to as earnings after taxes (EAT), the net income of the company after all taxes are calculated and deducted. In cases of larger companies, acquisitions are often continued as separate stand-alone enterprises. Therefore, the assumption is that taxation matters would not change, so the net income after taxes is the form of earnings preferred in the valuation.
- **Earnings before taxes (EBT):** For some large companies, the valuation is based on earnings before taxes (EBT), the net income without taxes being deducted. This may be a

preferred method if the taxation equation may change after a sale.

- **Earnings before interest and taxes (EBIT):** For others, it is based on earnings before interest and taxes (EBIT), the net income before taxes are deducted and with interest added back. In this case, there would be changes in the funding of the company, so the new funding costs would be considered separately.
- **Earnings before interest, taxes, depreciation, and amortization (EBITDA):** For middle-market-sized companies, the valuation is normally based on earnings before interest, taxes, depreciation, and amortization (EBITDA), or net income before taxes are deducted and with interest, depreciation, and amortization added back. Many practitioners say this definition of earnings is the most commonly used in business valuations. Other companies or private investment groups acquire many companies of this size. Taxes and funding costs would normally change after the acquisition.
- **Earnings before interest, taxes, depreciation, and amortization plus owner's compensation (EBITDA+OC):** For smaller businesses, value is typically based on cash flow, seller's discretionary earnings (SDE), or seller's cash flow (SCF), all of which are comparable to EBITDA plus owner's compensation (EBITDA+OC). Small business funding differs significantly for various companies and owners, and taxation varies considerably depending upon the type of legal entity and the participation of the owners.

## Determining Various Descriptions of Income

The following adjusted profit and loss statement provides an example of some possible methods of adjusting the financial statement to reflect the type of historical earnings important to certain types of buyers.

| **Chemical Company<br>Profit / (Loss)<br>2007–2010** | | | | |
|---|---|---|---|---|
| **Period** | **2007** | **2008** | **2009** | **2010** |
| **Sales** | **7,776,229** | **6,631,600** | **6,042,626** | **7,525,372** |
| Cost of goods sold | 5,143,823 | 4,432,789 | 3,949,355 | 4,922,734 |
| **Gross Profit** | **2,632,406** | **2,198,811** | **2,093,271** | **2,602,638** |
| Total operating expenses | 2,467,330 | 2,345,235 | 2,377,569 | 2,345,629 |
| **Net Operating Income** | **165,076** | **(146,424)** | **(284,298)** | **257,009** |
| Other income | 18,471 | 13,264 | 12,594 | |
| Less interest expense | (154,162) | (125,424) | (92,986) | |
| **Net Income before Taxes** | **24,178** | **(259,254)** | **(370,284)** | **168,955** |
| Interest expense | 154,162 | 125,424 | 92,986 | 88,054 |
| Other income | (13,264) | (12,594) | (7,000) | |
| Depreciation | 119,469 | 100,612 | 93,675 | 70,147 |
| Other financial exp. | 1,875 | 4,900 | 12,022 | 14,141 |
| Extraordinary legal | | | | 40,000 |
| State franchise tax | 800 | 800 | 800 | 800 |
| **Total Adjustments** | **263,042** | **219,142** | **192,483** | **213,142** |
| **EBITDA** | **287,220** | **(40,112)** | **(177,801)** | **382,097** |

The first section of this example reflects the gross revenue or total sales for each of four years, along with the total of cost of goods sold. Deducting the cost of goods sold from the gross sales gives us the gross profit margin. This is the margin of profit on sales that is available to pay the administrative and sales expenses and a net profit from the operation.

The next section of the complete statement shows a detailed list of administrative and sales expenses. The total of those expenses is shown in the above statement.

By deducting the operating expenses from the gross profit margin, we arrive at the net income from operations. From this figure, we deduct interest expense, which is not an operating expense, and we add back interest and rental income, which are nonoperational as well. This gives us the net income before taxes.

| **Net Income from Operations** | 165,076 | (146,424) | (284,298) | 257,009 |
|---|---|---|---|---|
| **Other Income:** | | | | |
| Rental income | 12,000 | 12,000 | 7,000 | |
| Interest income | 1,264 | 594 | | |
| **Total Other Income** | 18,471 | 13,264 | 12,594 | |
| **Subtotal Income** | 178,340 | (133,830) | (277,298) | 257,009 |
| **Less Interest Expense** | (154,162) | (125,424) | (92,986) | (88,054) |
| **Net Income before Taxes** | **24,178** | **(259,254)** | **(370,284)** | **168,955** |

In the next section, we review detailed adjustments to net income to arrive at the income category that is often preferred to be used in the determination of fair market value in a sale of the company.

You will note that interest expense is added back to income, as it is a cost of capital and not an operating expense. Other income is deducted, and the following is added back: depreciation, extraordinary legal expense, and state tax. These adjustments are normal adjustments in arriving at EBITDA.

| Adjustments: | | | | |
|---|---|---|---|---|
| Interest expense | 154,162 | 125,424 | 92,986 | 88,054 |
| Other income | (13,264) | (12,594) | (7,000) | |
| Depreciation | 119,469 | 100,612 | 93,675 | 70,147 |
| Other financial exp. | 1,875 | 4,900 | 12,022 | 14,141 |
| Extraordinary legal | | | | 40,000 |
| State franchise tax | 800 | 800 | 800 | 800 |
| **Total Adjustments** | 263,042 | 219,142 | 192,483 | 213,142 |
| **EBITDA** | **287,220** | **(40,112)** | **(177,801)** | **382,097** |

The reasoning for this evaluation of earnings is that taxation depends on many factors that are not directly related to earnings. Interest is a cost of capital, and it will vary with each potential owner and income. Expenses unrelated to the actual financial performance of the company have no effect on the potential performance of the business going forward.

If the desired category of earnings were preferred to be EBIT, then the interest and taxes would not be deducted from the earnings and would be added back to net income. If the desired income category were EBT, then taxes would not be deducted from the earnings. If the desired income category were EAT, nothing would be deducted in the equation. This earnings category would be net income after income taxes are deducted. If the desired income category were EBITDA+OC, the interest, taxes, depreciation, and amortization would not be deducted, and the owner's salary, benefits, and perquisites, adjusted to market, would be added back to the equation.

So as you can see, the adjusted income depends upon how the buyer, appraiser, or valuation analyst desires to interpret the income for the given valuation of the company and the particular use of the potential buyer. If new debt were funding the acquisition, the cost of the new debt would be factored into the total cost. If the seller were receiving a salary in excess of fair market value, the buyer would typically factor the excess into the valuation. The previous depreciation for taxation purposes of the seller would typically change for the buyer, so depreciation should be factored in as it would affect the buyer.

The above profit and loss statement was broken down and abbreviated for illustration purposes. The entire statement is shown here:

| Chemical Company<br>Profit / (Loss)<br>2006–2010 | | | | | |
|---|---|---|---|---|---|
| Period | | 2007 | 2008 | 2009 | 2010 |
| **Sales** | | **7,776,229** | **6,631,600** | **6,042,626** | **7,525,372** |
| **Cost of Goods Sold:** | | | | | |
| | Material | 3,051,542 | 2,541,712 | 2,729,003 | 3,697,104 |
| | Labor | 1,581,173 | 1,399,810 | 911,987 | 933,179 |
| | Depreciation | 119,469 | 100,612 | 93,675 | 79,147 |
| | Insurance | 81,783 | 130.769 | 22,500 | 37,351 |
| | Repairs and maintenance | 69,785 | 61,017 | 45,030 | 49,219 |
| | Supplies | 181,871 | 153,740 | 100,838 | 91,538 |
| | Taxes, licenses, permits | 48,186 | 27,948 | 29,916 | 23,842 |
| | Uniforms | 10,014 | 17,181 | 16,406 | 11,354 |
| **Total Cost of Goods Sold** | | 5,143,823 | 4,432,789 | 3,949,355 | 4,922,734 |
| | **Gross Profit** | **2,632,406** | **2,198,811** | **2,093,271** | **2,602,638** |
| **Expenses:** | | | | | |
| | Advertising | 22,269 | 38,379 | 6,512 | |
| | Automobile | 5,752 | 473 | 1,725 | 406 |
| | Bad debts | 19,881 | | 4,250 | 44,523 |
| | Bank charges | 1,168 | 4,927 | 9,493 | 5,132 |
| | Commission | 69,458 | 90,991 | 68,430 | 26,754 |
| | Consulting | 127,236 | 9,971 | 19,877 | 21,862 |
| | Dues and subscriptions | 18,412 | 3,852 | 2,913 | 3,497 |
| | Employee benefits | 13,553 | 6,143 | 2,344 | |
| | Freight | 145,895 | 129,088 | | |
| | Insurance | 44,816 | 107,334 | 104,053 | 33,922 |

| | | | | | |
|---|---|---|---|---|---|
| | Legal and accounting | 22,652 | 37,714 | 30,993 | 73,645 |
| | Miscellaneous | 2,438 | 262 | 7,292 | 135 |
| | Office expense | 27,907 | 27,578 | 2,435 | 2,918 |
| | Office salaries | 1,032,832 | 897,601 | 1,099,705 | 1,106,372 |
| | Officers' salaries | 136,450 | 229,680 | 221,468 | 277,054 |
| | Other financial expenses | 1,875 | 4,900 | 12,022 | 14,141 |
| | Payroll preparation fees | 4,651 | 5,423 | 5,418 | 6,392 |
| | Payroll tax expense | 102,236 | 92,962 | 81,191 | 97,415 |
| | Rent | 409,363 | 357,412 | 354,072 | 364,692 |
| | Repairs and maintenance | 53,762 | 45,776 | 41,626 | 41,845 |
| | Taxes, licenses, permits | 14,009 | 14,341 | 14,771 | 15,108 |
| | Telephone | 27,995 | 18,637 | 25,181 | 17,758 |
| | Travel | 32,556 | 13,328 | 9,173 | 1,551 |
| | Utilities | 83,617 | 83,578 | 89,855 | 91,283 |
| | Workers comp. insurance | | | 38,403 | 83,863 |
| **Total Expenses** | | **2,467,330** | **2,345,235** | **2,377,569** | **2,345,629** |
| **Net Income from Operations** | | **165,076** | **(146,424)** | **(284,298)** | **257,009** |
| **Other Income:** | | | | | |
| | Rental income | 12,000 | 12,000 | 7,000 | |
| | Interest income | 1,264 | 594 | | |
| **Total Other Income** | | 18,471 | 13,264 | 12,594 | |
| **Subtotal Income** | | 178,340 | (133,830) | (277,298) | 257,009 |
| **Less Interest Expense** | | (154,162) | (125,424) | (92,986) | (88,054) |
| **Net Income before Taxes** | | **24,178** | **(259,254)** | **(370,284)** | **168,955** |
| **Adjustments:** | | | | | |
| | Interest expense | 154,162 | 125,424 | 92,986 | 88,054 |
| | Other income | (13,264) | (12,594) | (7,000) | |
| | Depreciation | 119,469 | 100,612 | 93,675 | 70,147 |
| | Other financial exp. | 1,875 | 4,900 | 12,022 | 14,141 |
| | Extraordinary legal | | | | 40,000 |
| | State franchise tax | 800 | 800 | 800 | 800 |
| **Total Adjustments** | | 263,042 | 219,142 | 192,483 | 213,142 |
| **EBITDA** | | | | **(177,801)** | **382,097** |

## Discretionary Earnings

For smaller businesses, cash flow is just what its name implies, the cash that will flow into the owner's pocket, the amount of earnings that the owner could spend with complete discretion, the amount not needed to keep the company running but could be extracted for personal use. For smaller businesses, this would include the salary of the owner, any benefits and perquisites received by the owner, and the net earnings of the business after all expenses are deducted. This is often referred to as seller's cash flow, discretionary earnings, or seller's discretionary earnings (SDE), which is usually equivalent to the equation above defined as EBITDA+OC. Owner's compensation includes not only salary and benefits but perquisites as well. Perquisites would include any expenses included as business expenses that are not necessary for the operation of the business, such as automobiles, country clubs, vacation homes, home improvements, boats, motor homes, entertainment, and many others.

Many adjustments can be made with authenticity to increase or decrease the actual cash flow, but the bottom line times the multiple of earnings selected, with some justification, will ultimately determine the estimated value using this method of valuation.

The method of determining net income and the adjustments made to determine cash flow are arguable, but this basic way of looking at the price that a buyer could justify is often considered to be the most reasonable assessment of a prudent investment.

Arguments can be made for adding back amortization and depreciation, noncash expenses. They were cash expenses at one time, so one could argue that they should be considered an actual expense at some point. However, if you buy the business, you probably will not incur these expenses again. The buyer's capitalization of the acquisition may provide the buyer with amortization and depreciation, which may reduce buyer's future taxation and should then be considered in the equation of the transaction and valuation. An argument could also be made that equipment and fixtures that are acquired will have to be replaced at some point, so an allowance for replacement may be necessary in the equation.

These are all valid points but often overlooked in the valuation of a small business, particularly because of the short future duration one is willing to consider as a reasonable period of sustainability of earnings. The following are other considerations:

- possible adjustments to market value, such as owner's salary, which is above or below market
- inventory changes not reflected in the cost of goods sold
- bad debts
- adjustments to market rent for rent paid to the company owner for the business premises, which can be either below or above market rate for the area where the company is located

For a simple example of adjustments to determine discretionary earnings, we can use a profit and loss statement from a small business that illustrates the calculation of discretionary earnings as well as other income and expense items that should be considered in determining the value of the business. In this first section, we show gross sales, less cost of goods sold, and gross profit.

| Ice Cream Shop<br>Profit/(Loss)<br>2007–2008–2009 | | | |
|---|---|---|---|
| | 2007 | 2008 | 2009 |
| **Sales** | 202,911 | 241,619 | 182,355 |
| Cost of goods sold | (34,348) | (41,793) | (32,456) |
| **Gross Profit** | 168,563 | 199,826 | 149,899 |

The next section shows an itemization of operating expenses, which gives us net operating income after deducting them from gross profit.

| **Expenses** | | | | |
|---|---|---|---|---|
| | Advertising and promotion | 1,291 | 5,421 | 420 |
| | Amortization | 1,030 | 5,116 | |
| | Auto expense | 1,049 | 7,806 | 5,249 |
| | Bank charges | 350 | 2,897 | 1,969 |
| | Contributions | 410 | 2,070 | |
| | Depreciation | 7,758 | 46,223 | 9,455 |
| | Insurance-Liability | 2,819 | 9,303 | 3,154 |
| | Insurance-Health | 2,024 | 4,862 | 2,000 |
| | Interest | 3,400 | 22,611 | 3,265 |
| | Laundry and uniforms | 700 | 681 | 344 |
| | Licenses and permits | 1,191 | 2,100 | 1,611 |
| | Miscellaneous | 92 | 343 | 542 |
| | Office supplies | 318 | 1,240 | 1,724 |
| | Outside services | 270 | 764 | 227 |
| | Payroll | 18,017 | 28,759 | 8,866 |

| | | | |
|---|---|---|---|
| Payroll taxes | 2,105 | 3,296 | 1,091 |
| Professional fees | 750 | 3,093 | 675 |
| Rent | 11,061 | 34,300 | 25,195 |
| Repairs and maintenance | 126 | 2,336 | 308 |
| Royalties | 8,567 | 12,542 | |
| Security | 565 | 997 | |
| Supplies | 5,176 | 19,094 | |
| Telephone and Internet | 1,987 | 3,966 | 2,039 |
| Travel and entertainment | | 534 | 329 |
| Utilities | 1,690 | 10,294 | 4,120 |
| **Total Expenses** | **74,746** | **230,648** | **72,583** |
| **Net Operating Income** | 93,817 | (30,822) | 77,316 |

From net operating income, we make normal and necessary adjustments to arrive at discretionary earnings.

| **Adjustments** | — | | |
|---|---|---|---|
| Amortization | 1,030 | 5,116 | |
| Contributions | 2,410 | 2,070 | |
| Depreciation | 7,758 | 6,223 | 9,455 |
| Interest | 3,400 | 22,611 | 3,265 |
| Personal auto use | 500 | 3,900 | 2,600 |
| **Total Adjustments** | **15,098** | **79,920** | **15,320** |
| **Discretionary Earnings** | 108,915 | 49,098 | 92,636 |

Amortization, depreciation, and contributions are added back as nonoperational expenses, interest is added back as a cost of capital, and personal auto use is added back as a perquisite for the business owner, a nonoperational expense.

## Other Value Considerations

Other items in the above income statement are worthy of consideration in determining value as well:

- Sales were down in 2009, probably due to the economic recession. If this can be verified, one may be safe in not fully considering that year in the calculation of average cash flow. But perhaps a different reason should be explained in determining earnings.
- Payroll declined substantially in 2009, a factor that may have required the owners to work more hours and to have reduced hours for employees. In a typical valuation, only the employment of one owner working a normal schedule is considered as owner compensation. Any additional labor contributed by the owners should probably be added in as an expense, thereby reducing the earnings and the value computation.
- No royalty was paid to the franchisor during 2009, and no supplies were purchased, both of which would require the owner's explanation for accurate consideration in the calculation and possible addition to expenses for the year.

## Multiples of Earnings

The term, "multiples of earnings," refers to the number of years of the company's historical earnings considered to be appropriate to determine value. You could define it as the number of years in which a prudent buyer would expect to receive a return of the total purchase price of the company through the expected earnings. This period selected will vary with the size of the company, the strategy of the buyer, the industry trends, the financial strength, and the anticipated sustainability of earnings.

Multiples of earnings as a method of determining value can be a somewhat nebulous subject. Historical records of small business sales would probably reflect a multiple of 1.5 to 3 times discretionary earnings as the common pricing of a small business, as reported by the *Valuing Small Businesses and Professional Practices* authored by Shannon Pratt, Robert Reilly, and Robert P. Schweihs. Previous speakers at conferences I have attended have indicated the average multiple of earnings for the sale of small businesses is 2.2 times. In my own practice of sale transactions, I can report multiples of earnings from less than one times earnings to twelve times earnings for small companies. All of these, however, merely indicate businesses in general and should not be accepted as a proven method of pricing a company. Too many factors can affect value determination and increase or decrease the fair market value of a business.

If we look at the earnings of the above example and decide a reasonable price for this company is 2.5 times the historical earnings, the value could be estimated to be about $200,000. We could assume many different acquisition structures in analyzing this pricing as a way of determining the accuracy of such pricing.

# CHAPTER 5

## *Questions to Consider in Determining Value*

Some factors that are important to consider in your valuation equation may be:

- Is the business being operated efficiently now?
- Has it reached its potential of profitability?
- Is the neighborhood getting better or worse?
- Is the industry getting better or worse?
- Is there a possibility that business will decline when the owner walks out the door?

All of these considerations and others should become a part of the calculation in determining the value of the business.

### Comparing Acquisition Cost with a Start-Up

When considering the value of the business, one might look at it from the perspective of a potential buyer and consider the cost of starting this business anew and developing it to the point that has now been achieved.

What would be the start-up costs? How long would it take to establish enough business to be profitable? One way of looking at the value would be to consider the initial investment, the earnings during the start-up and development stages, the amount of time it may require to reach the current income level, and the possibility of failure. These numbers could add up to a much larger number than the cost of acquiring this business that has already proven to be a viable enterprise.

If it will require capital of $100,000 to start the business and will take two years before making a profit and the buyer's income requirement is $60,000 annually, then the initial cost will be $220,000. This is assuming that the buyer can generate enough business to achieve these assumptions. Using a comparison such as this can help to justify the value of a business.

Suppose the buyer borrows the $220,000 and the debt service of the loan will be $30,000 annually. This will typically require gross sales of $150,000 or more just to satisfy the debt service before any profit could be allocated to owner compensation. Will a buyer feel comfortable with accepting that challenge? Or would it be more comfortable to buy the business that already has a proven profitably? All of these considerations are important in evaluating a company for sale purposes.

## Sanity Test

Some of those involved in evaluating and selling businesses like to use what is sometimes referred to as a sanity test. Hereby you would assume the role of the buyer and simply determine the income of the business or the income that you feel confident can be achieved. You deduct the following items:

- the personal income that the buyer would require from the business income

- the debt service that will be incurred in acquiring the business from the income
- a reasonable rate of return that would be expected from any down payment made for the acquisition from the income
- any additional immediate costs that will be incurred over some reasonable period of time from the income

A sanity test might look something like this:

| Sale Price | 350,000 | Gross Earnings | 700,000 |
|---|---|---|---|
| Acquisition financing | 250,000 | Cost of sales | (450,000) |
| 7.5 percent loan over ten years | | Expenses | (100,000) |
| SBA or seller financing | | Cash flow | 150,000 |
| Down payment | 100,000 | Owner's salary | (100,000) |
| Working capital | 70,000 | Debt service | (25,000) |
| Projected improvements | 10,000 | Return on investment | (10,000) |
| Total Cash Requirement | 180,000 | Net Cash Flow | 15,000 |

The above is merely an example of a way to determine how a potential buyer of your business may evaluate the sanity of the acquisition—whether the acquisition makes sense or not. These numbers or this method are not a recommendation of a viable acquisition but merely an indication of how a decision might be based.

It is important to remember that, in the sale of small businesses, the seller often retains the cash, cash equivalents, and accounts receivable. Therefore, the buyer must calculate the infusion of working capital into the equation of cash required. Working capital, of course, is the day-to-day cash required to make payroll and other expenses until customer payment of sales or services are received. This requirement will vary with different types of businesses. Businesses that allow thirty-day payment for invoices must have working capital to finance these outstanding receivables, which should be more than one month's average sales. A stable business should always have some excess cash on hand to cover unexpected events that may occur. After a company has been in business for a number of years, lines of credit from local banks are usually available for such contingencies, but in the initial stages, it is imperative for the buyer to have cash on hand, so the seller should consider this requirement in evaluating the company.

In the above example, the return on invested cash is 8.3 percent, the total cash flow is $150,000, including owner compensation of $100,000, and the purchase price is 2.3 times discretionary cash flow. Are these performance estimates sufficient to make the acquisition feasible for the buyer? This is an example of a sanity test as support for other valuation methods.

The subject business has average annual gross revenue of $750,000 for several years. The company has seller's discretionary earnings of $150,000. This, of course, includes net income before taxes, owner's salary, and any perquisites and benefits the owner receives. The sale price for the business is $250,000. The working capital the buyer must provide is estimated at $80,000.

Based upon this, the owner will pay all liabilities and retain the cash and cash equivalent assets. This amounts to $70,000. There is $30,000 in accounts payable and no bank debt or other liabilities. So, under this scenario, the owner would receive a total net amount of $290,000 ($250,000 + $70,000 – $30,000), less any escrow or broker fees.

The buyer could be looking at various financing scenarios:

| Business Acquisition—Sanity Test | |
|---|---|
| Acquisition cost | $250,000 |
| Down payment @ 20 percent | 50,000 |
| Financing required | 200,000 |
| Terms: 10 years @ 7.5 percent | |
| Working capital required | 80,000 |
| **Total Cash Investment** | **$130,000** |
| Gross sales of the company | $750,000 |
| Anticipated earnings of company | 150,000 |
| Acquisition financing debt service | (30,000) |
| Annual improvements required | (10,000) |
| Return on cash investment | (13,000) |
| **Balance—Owner's Discretionary Earnings** | **$97,000** |

| Business Acquisition—Sanity Test | |
|---|---|
| Acquisition cost | $250,000 |
| Down payment @ 100 percent | 250,000 |
| Financing required | |
| Terms: 10 years @ 7.5 percent | |
| Working capital required | 80,000 |
| **Total Cash Investment** | **$330,000** |
| Gross sales of the company | $750,000 |
| Anticipated earnings of company | 150,000 |
| Acquisition financing debt service | |
| Annual improvements required | (10,000) |
| Return on cash investment | (33,000) |
| **Balance—Owner's Discretionary Earnings** | **$107,000** |

| Business Acquisition—Sanity Test | |
|---|---|
| Acquisition cost | $250,000 |
| Down payment @ 40 percent | 100,000 |
| Financing required | 150,000 |
| Terms: 10 years @ 7.5 percent | |
| Working capital required | 80,000 |
| **Total Cash Investment** | **180,000** |
| Gross sales of the company | $750,000 |
| Anticipated earnings of the company | 150,000 |
| Acquisition financing debt service | (22,000) |
| Annual improvements required | (10,000) |
| Return on cash investment | (18,000) |
| **Balance—Owner's Discretionary Earnings** | **$100,000** |

In analyzing the sanity of this acquisition, we should consider some questions:

- What is the risk of failure?
- Can the business be expanded?
- Are the annual earnings sufficient for the buyer?
- Is the debt nonrecourse?
- Would seller financing make more sense for the buyer or the seller?
- Does the future of the industry look promising?
- Is the return on invested cash sufficient for the risk?

Questions such as this can be important considerations in acquisition negotiations and the agreement on the value of the enterprise. They can support a buyer's decision to buy or decline and/or the seller's decision to proceed or retain the company.

## Risk Adjustment or Risk Premium

Every investment has a level of risk of failure or diminishing returns. The lowest risk level is normally considered to be US Treasury Bills, which are generally considered risk-free. Any other investment should receive an adjustment of what is called a risk premium or risk adjustment. This is an adjustment to compensate the buyer for the risk of not receiving a full return of the investment. A Fortune 500 company would receive a risk adjustment on the low side due to the size, stability, tenure, and financial soundness. A small business, due to the fragile nature of small businesses, would generally receive a higher risk adjustment.

A recent survey of market risk premium, "Market Risk Premium Used in 82 countries in 2012: A Survey with 7,192 Answers," conducted by Pablo Fernandez, Javier Aguirreamalloa, and Luis Corres, IESE Business School, University of Navarra, reflected a premium average of 5.5 percent over the risk-free rate for US public companies in 2013. The rate for the long US Treasury Bond is, at the time of this writing, quoted at 2.6 percent. This is often referred to as the risk-free rate. The risk premium would indicate that, because a risk-free rate of return is 2.6 percent, the market risk rate of return for US public companies, on average, is 8.1 percent.

This risk adjustment is expected for the largest companies on the stock market. From this, one could extrapolate a rate for smaller companies much higher, such rates as high as 50 percent for small businesses. This helps to explain the valuation of smaller companies at 1.5 to 3.0 times earnings as opposed to large corporations that could sell for 10 to 100 times earnings on the stock market or in a buyout of a public company.

## Market Comparisons

Sale prices of comparable companies are often used as a method of supporting valuations and asking prices of businesses. Such information is available through various sources, such as the Institute of Business Appraisers (go-iba.org), Bizcomps (bizcomps.com), and Pratt Stats (bvmarketdata.com). Available online, these organizations are accessible by those subscribing to the use of their data. These comparisons can often assist in determination of the sanity of a pricing decision.

In performing market comparisons for a basis of pricing, it is important to remember to compare apples to apples as much as possible. The industry should be comparable to the subject company, the size should be similar, the geographic area may be important, the product lines should be comparable, and risk factors may be important. Many other factors should be considered when basing pricing on selected comparables.

## Rules of Thumb

Rules of thumb are often used in pricing small businesses. Rules of thumb come about by experience in the transfer of companies in various industries. For instance, some franchises typically sell for prices based on certain multiples of sales, and some automobile service stations may sell for prices based on gallons of gas sold monthly or annually. Brokers who specialize in specific industries for long periods of time sometimes determine rules of thumb for their industry. The Business Brokerage Press in Worcester, Massachusetts (businessbrokeragepress.com), has published *Business Reference Guide* for many years. The book provides data on the sale of small companies, and it grows in size and number of entries each year and contains rules of thumb for hundreds of categories of businesses. These are primarily small businesses, as larger businesses would typically need a more comprehensive basis for a valuation.

Hundreds of these are available in the *Business Reference Guide*, but they are just what they say, rules of thumb. No consideration is given for the duration of the company, the growth potential, the desirability of location, the financing alternatives, or the sustainability of earnings. Rules of thumb can be used as a pricing source or support for valuations calculated on earnings. They are based on the experience of brokers or trade groups from various industries who have knowledge of numerous business transfers in their specialties.

## Size Matters

The size of a company has a definite effect on business valuation and the sale price of a business. The smaller a company, the more fragile it usually is. In other words, the smaller it is, the less adversity it would take to make it fail. The smaller it is, the higher the cost of capital, either invested or borrowed. Because of these factors, the smaller the company, the lower the multiple of earnings that it would typically sell for. A Fortune 500 company might sell its stock at a 10 to 100 times earnings, or price-to-earnings ratio (PE ratio). Few small companies could support a 10-to-1 ratio. A small business that sells for $100,000 might represent a sale price of 1.5 times earnings. A small business that sells for $500,000 may represent a sale price of 2.5 times earnings. These numbers will vary depending on the many other factors that we have discussed; however, size does matter. That is what is meant by the following terms: risk premium, risk discount, or risk adjustment. Size and financial stability matter.

## Other Value Drivers

Although the more easily recognized values of a business are the earnings, some of the less obvious assets and qualities are sometimes more important to certain potential buyers and can increase or decrease the value of your business. These could include:

- **Highly skilled employees:** Tool and die makers, web designers, chefs, medical technicians, engineers, sales professionals, and other acquired skills and levels of education
- **Trade secrets:** Special processes, patents, and copyrights
- **Reputation:** Well known and respected in the given industry or area, enabling expansion
- **Special facilities:** High-tech equipment, proprietary tooling, or specific facilities for an industry
- **Special location:** A certain street, corner, neighborhood, or retail center
- **Growing industry:** An industry with new technology or a trendy and popular product line
- **Licensing:** Limited licensing in certain industries or products, such as liquor or FDA licenses
- **Distribution rights:** Brand-name merchandise with limited distribution rights
- **Designs:** Patented or copyrighted designs
- **Copyrights:** Copyrights for formulas or literature
- **Barriers to entry:** Large investment requirement in facilities, licensing restrictions, technology requirements, or limitation on new start-ups

## Consolidation of Companies

Value can be enhanced for certain companies in an acquisition by a competitive firm or another existing company in a merger of operations. In a merger or consolidation of operations, there can sometimes be significant savings of operational expenses by eliminating duplicate staffing or excess facilities or performing functions in-house that were formerly outsourced at a higher cost by one firm or the other. Perhaps the existing sales staff can handle the additional product lines or services, or maybe one firm or the other may have excess capacity for housing or production. There may be opportunities to add services in both companies by cross marketing of customer bases. There may be pricing advantages by eliminating a competitor. There may be special processes or other advantages that could add up to, what some say, 1 + 1 = 3.

The above value drivers are often referred to as strategies or synergies and can be just as, or more, valuable than any other considerations.

# CHAPTER 6

## *Other Factors Affecting Valuation*

Valuation of companies can be a straightforward process. It is with most small companies. It can also become quite complex. *Valuing Small Businesses and Professional Practices* only covers the market approach to valuation. Not included was the asset or income approach. Those would entail two more books of the same size.

### Valuation for Litigation

The subject of valuation can get very complex when it involves valuing businesses for litigation, where business dissolutions between partners or spouses are being argued. Some of the complexity arises when a valuation is market based, whereby studies of prior sales of businesses are used for comparison of values and adjustments are made to every phase of the financial and operational aspects of the targeted business.

When court testimony is required from experts in the field, it is necessary for these experts to demonstrate their positions with facts and figures and formulas, a very expensive process. The specialists in this field are well compensated and must earn their fees with industry statistics and market studies.

These practices are not necessary when it comes to forming an opinion of value on a small company for arriving at a sale price that makes sense for a buyer and adequately compensates the seller for the asset being sold. In cases of litigation, situations where experts get involved, we are really talking about business appraisals performed by established experts in the field.

## Distressed Companies

Companies with financial difficulties also have value, although they perhaps cannot be expressed in the same format as profitable, growing concerns. The market for such companies is limited compared with profitable, growing companies.

It is not at all uncommon for small and large companies to have periods of losses, liquidity problems, lack of ability to service debts, and insufficient access to capital to sustain viability. There are various alternatives, of course, to cure or deal with such deficiencies—new sources of capital or management, renegotiation of debt, consultation of industry experts, sale of the company, a merger with competitors, a downsize of operations, a divest of divisions, workout plans with creditors, liquidation, or bankruptcy.

In any of these possible solutions, there could be significant value in the company or salvageable operations or assets. Such value could be present in special facilities, machinery and equipment, proprietary product lines, special tooling or processes, access to customers, trained employees, experienced management, patents, copyrights, and reputation. Any or all of these assets could have value to an acquirer and could lead to a favorable disposition of the company.

Whether a company is profitable or distressed, valuation is an important early step in the process of a successful transfer of the company.

## Sources of Education for Appraisal or Valuation

### The Institute of Businesses Appraisers (www.go-iba.org)

This firm provides a course of study for the business appraisal industry, which requires several years of study and testing to become a Certified Business Appraiser. Very few transactions of small businesses changing hands ever require the services of an appraiser with credentials from companies that certify their expertise.

### The International Business Brokers Association (www.IBBA.org)

This association provides a course of study and offers credentials as a Certified Business Intermediary. This very thorough and professional training is generally sufficient to qualify brokers for valuation of small businesses.

### Some State Business Broker Associations

These associations also offer education and certification for those who make a career in the transfer of business enterprises. California offers the California Association of Business Brokers (www.CABB.org), and Texas offers the Texas Association of Business Brokers (www.TABB.org). Many others can be contacted through the IBBA (www.IBBA.org).

### The M&A Source (www.masource.org)

This association provides a course of study and offers credentials as a Mergers & Acquisitions Master Intermediary. This comprehensive and professional training is generally sufficient to qualify intermediaries for valuation and transfer of middle-market-sized companies.

You are able to select whatever method and level of valuation you feel comfortable with when preparing your business for sale. You can pay nothing for an opinion, or you can pay $50,000 for an appraisal and marketing platform. The important fact to remember is that you are really selling future income and the buyer must be able to understand the value and feel comfortable that it will provide a future source of income that supports the sale price.

## Case Study: Unreasonable Expectations in Valuation

I was engaged as a business advisor for a manufacturer of skin care and hygienic products, in which a gentleman of retirement age had majority ownership. He was seeking an exit from the company with some comfortable means of retirement. A brief review of the information provided indicated the need for a valuation to be completed. Upon completion of a valuation, the owner was advised that, due to the reduced sales and earnings in the previous two years and the heavy debt owed to banks and others, it would be difficult to sell the company for a price that would achieve his objective. The expected sale price, after retiring all debt and other financial obligations, was not considered to be sufficient to fulfill the objectives of the equity owners of the company.

The owners considered this advice briefly and decided that they wished to offer the company to market regardless of this advice. Because they were willing to provide the up-front cost of marketing the company and this type of company with exceptional facilities and capacity sometimes attracts a seller willing to make a sale work due to specific strategic considerations, we proceeded with an offering of the company.

Once the materials were prepared and the offering was advertised, the process generated more than four hundred leads and interested parties over a period of many months. As the owners were advised, attraction of an acceptable offer to purchase was difficult due to the company's fluctuating earnings and the heavy debt load.

Several offers to purchase were received. These offers were all based on a valuation of the historical earnings of the company, and the seller rejected them all because they were insufficient to retire the company's debts and fund the majority owner's retirement.

Eventually, a buyer who was willing to pay the premium required in spite of having little assurance of a reasonable return on investment stepped forward. A contract was negotiated, and due diligence began. Due diligence was soon completed, but the loan commitment, a contingency of the sale, was not forthcoming. The obstacle to a loan commitment was the overpricing of the business. The historical earnings would not support debt service of the purchase financing required to consummate the acquisition.

The company was manufacturing and packaging a product for a customer using the customer's proprietary product formula and compound. Under this situation, a manufacturer and packager is expected, generally agrees, and is sometimes legally obligated to protect the customer's proprietary rights to the intellectual property.

Another customer approached the company desiring a similar product. The owners changed the formula slightly and packaged the product for the new customer. The customer who owned the formula found out about the sale to the new customer and alleged infringement of his proprietary rights. Legal action ensued. A trial of the case finally transpired. Unfortunately for the owners, the customer with the allegedly infringed proprietary rights won a judgment of several million dollars against the company.

This judgment being greater than the value of the company, the company was forced into bankruptcy and liquidated in its entirety. The sale of the company provided no retirement funds for the majority owner or any return of equity capital to minority owners.

This unfortunate ending can be traced back to one point, unreasonable expectations. If the earnings had supported the sale price, the buyer would have been able to get his financing, and the sale could have been consummated.

So the lesson should be to get as good a valuation as possible and price the company accordingly. Trying to force a sale at a price that cannot be supported not only makes a sale unlikely but interferes with the successful management of your business.

# CHAPTER 7

## *Preparing the Company for Sale*

### Get It Ready to Sell

Preparation of the company for sale is an important early stage of the sale process. Preparation can make a big difference in the presentation of your company. The saying "You only get one chance to make a first impression" is a good way to approach the essential step of getting your company ready to sell and show and getting it ready for a new owner.

### Showtime Readiness

A used car dealer provides a good example of getting it ready to sell. When car dealers prepare to sell used cars, what is the first thing they do? They make sure they are in as good condition as possible and buyers will feel the assurance of good, reliable transportation and there will be no problem with ownership. They touch up all chips and scratches. They install new tires if necessary. They buff, polish, and clean every inch of every car. They shampoo the carpets and replace the floor mats. They clean the engines. They make sure the mufflers are good and the cars run quietly. They get them ready to sell. That is what should be done with your business. A prospective new owner should feel comfortable that your business will provide his or her need and the profitability and success is transferable and sustainable.

Did you ever walk into a local business and feel like this would be a good place to work? Your business should look and feel like this, a good place to work. You should make sure your facilities are as a presentable as possible. You should make sure everything looks orderly and well managed.

You should also make sure that all of the other factors that would make it a good place to work are represented as well, such as customer relations, employee relations, integrity, quality of products and services, and reputation in the industry and community.

## Financial Readiness

One of the most important preparations is getting the financial information in order. Get together with your accountant and make sure all of your financial statements and tax returns are complete and accurate so they can be produced when requested and are easy to understand. Make sure your sales records are complete and self-explanatory. Prepare lists of the production equipment, office equipment and furnishings, and transportation equipment. Prepare a summary of inventory if it is critical to the operation.

## Operational Readiness

Operational readiness should include the launching of expansion programs, if possible. This will help to convince the potential buyer that expansion is in the works and growth is achievable.

- If you have a transportation company, make sure all of your vehicles are in good repair. Make sure the drivers will impress a potential buyer with a professional manner of your operation. Make sure you are state-of-the-art equipped in order to be competitive in price and quality.
- If you have a manufacturing company, make sure you have a well-trained and qualified staff. Make sure the shop is well organized for an efficient operation. Make sure the machinery and equipment are in good operating condition.
- If you have a plumbing company, make sure the trucks are in good repair and the technicians are proficient, punctual, and well mannered.

## Legal Readiness

If you lease your property, be sure your lease is assignable. Extend your lease or negotiate an option to extend, if possible. Many businesses depend upon their location or the type of facilities they occupy. If the location is important to the success of the business and there is no assurance that it can continue for a good length of time, either the value diminishes considerably or it is impossible to sell.

## Employee Readiness

Correct any employee deficiencies that may exist. Disgruntled or unqualified employees are a hindrance for you in operating the company and will interfere in selling it. Resolve personnel problems of inefficiency, poor attendance, or personality conflicts. If there is a problem of high turnover, you should determine the reason: undesirable type of work, insufficient pay, or a difficult employee. If you have a key employee that the business depends upon for a large part of its success, get an employment agreement, or at least make sure the employee will stay on with a new owner.

## Customer Readiness

If you have a limited customer base with one customer or a small number of customers who represent a large portion of your business, try to expand your customer base. This is most important and should be done well in advance of offering your company to market. The customer base is critical for the buyer to succeed, and it should be well established for assurance of sustainability. A company with a large portion of the business concentrated in one or a few customers, sometimes referred to as "too many eggs in one basket," is considered fragile because the loss of one or more customers could be devastating for the company. These situations can reduce the value significantly or render the business not saleable.

Companies with steady growth in revenue and earnings are more desirable than those with income fluctuations or level income year after year. Such a pattern indicates an inability to grow the company. This phase, like most all of the others, depends upon the type of business and the size of the business.

## Case History: Preparing for the Sale

The following case provides an example of what can happen when you really have nothing to sell:

> I was engaged to sell a company selling and installing glass, mirrors, shower enclosures, and other bath accessories.

The owner was of retirement age and wanted to move to another state. The company was profitable. The business primarily was generated through clients that the owner knew personally and one elderly independent sales representative who supplied her with additional work to sustain profitability. She offered the business for sale at a price that was reasonable based on her current income. There were no offers for an outright acquisition of the company, but numerous interested parties expressed a desire to take over the company and continue to operate it on an earn-out basis, whereby a small down payment would be made and the seller would receive payment of a percentage of the income for a specified period of years. The reason for this structure was that the income depended too much upon the current owner's relationships and a limited sales effort by a retirement-age independent representative.

She declined this sale structure because of the uncertainty of receiving additional value from the company. Because she had decided to discontinue her operation of the business, she had declined to renew her lease for the property. Consequently, the property owner sold the building and gave her notice to move.

Because she had already begun her relocation to another state to live, she chose to liquidate the company. She liquidated the remaining assets, including the service truck, furnishings, and shop equipment and ended up with very little value for the company even though it had previously produced a good income.

What steps should the owner have taken to make the company saleable?

- She should have made the company ready to sell.
- She should have expanded her customer base with more local customers.
- She should have renewed her lease to assure a continuation of the company at its current location.
- She should have increased the volume of business in order to give a potential buyer enough confidence to offer more attractive terms of sale, terms that would have assured her with a price certain rather than a percentage of future sales.
- She should have agreed to stay on for a specified period in order to help the buyer retain the customer base and become fully acclimated in the business.

I advised her of all of these important steps; however, she was anxious to move on and unwilling to prepare the company for sale. As it turned out, she had nothing to sell.

## Case History: A Company Well Prepared for Sale

This case emphasizes the importance of being ready to sell in all categories:

> My firm had a business representation agreement to find a buyer for an automotive shop in the Los Angeles area. The

shop had been in business under the same ownership for fifteen years. They had good financial statements reflecting steady growth during the previous four years. The total revenue was $650,000. Discretionary earnings were reported as $125,000. The owner intended to return to his home country.

The shop was up-to-date with state-of-the-art equipment. It was clean, recently painted, and orderly. The business was located on a major thoroughfare in a well-populated area. Approximately 20 percent of the shop's business was provided from a used car lot next door and a neighborhood independent car rental company. The remainder came from returning customers and new customers attracted from the good signage, some local advertising, and word of mouth. The facility's lease had nearly five years remaining and a five-year option with a rent escalation and was assignable.

The company was advertised and had numerous inquiries from interested parties.

One inquirer had considerable experience in auto repair. He had previously owned a shop in another state and had a down payment of about half of the purchase price. The owner's bank was willing to provide the necessary financing providing the seller would carry 10 percent of the purchase price. The seller agreed, and the deal was done.

> The seller agreed to stay on for thirty to sixty days for training, transition assistance, and conveyance of the regular customer base for the satisfaction of the new owner. The sale price was $275,000 with a $135,000 down payment, a bank loan of $112,500, and a seller note of $27,500. The company was earning $125,000 annually. The debt service for the five-year loan was approximately $25,000 annually. The seller note payments were approximately $6,500 annually. The buyer's income requirement was $70,000. The numbers worked. The seller walked with $247,500, less selling fees and costs, and was to receive $6,500 annually for five years. The buyer paid down $135,000, provided $40,000 in working capital to operate the company, and had a company that provided a great deal of assurance of a continuing stream of income.

This company was showtime, financially, operationally, employee, customer, and legally ready to sell. Both the buyer and seller were ready, willing, and able. A mutually beneficial transaction was consummated amiably and professionally.

# CHAPTER 8

## *Offering the Company for Sale*

### The Method of Offering

A professional in the business of selling businesses, such as a business broker, business intermediary, real estate broker, merger and acquisition intermediary, attorney at law, or investment banker can offer your company for sale. Or you can make the offering as for sale by owner. The advantages and disadvantages of the method you choose are important to consider.

If you choose a for-sale-by-owner approach, the advantages may be tighter control of confidentiality, dissemination of information, and negotiations; no advance fees for preparation and offering; no commission on the sale price; and ability to remove the offering at any time. The disadvantages may be inexperience in handling such a transaction, consumption-of-time strains on management, and absence of professional advice in preparation and negotiations.

If you choose a professional in the business of selling businesses approach, the advantages may be expertise in preparation of information, marketing the offering, and negotiations, and possible buyer prospects that the professional or his or her associates may be aware of. The disadvantages may be lack of control over confidentiality; possible lack of effort by the chosen professional; cost of preparation, marketing, and cost of commission on sale; and legal responsibility to the professional.

Many company owners choose to use the services of a professional to sell their companies because of the expertise gained in preparation, marketing, negotiation, and closing the transaction. However, owners sell many companies without a professional involved, except in closing the transaction.

A company owner can prepare the company for sale, advertise it, communicate with interested parties, negotiate the transaction, and close the sale without any assistance, except what state law may require. Some states require an attorney to close a transaction. Some states allow closings to be done by escrow agents, similar to real estate sales.

## Some Legal Requirements

Most states consider small business asset sales as bulk sale transactions. These transactions must usually be closed through an escrow agent who orders searches for outstanding debts and obligations, gets tax clearances from governmental agencies, advertises the sale as required by state law, prepares all of the documents (promissory notes, bills of sale, and Uniform Commercial Code [UCC] filings for fixtures and equipment), and closing statements for buyer and seller.

In most states, the transaction must be advertised in a legal publication for a period of time for the benefit of any creditor who may be unaware of the sale. These transfers are subject to the state's UCC with appropriate legal filings to protect the lender's interests in the assets and to protect the buyer from claims by undisclosed creditors. The sale closings of smaller businesses are rather simple to consummate, but the larger the business, the more imperative it is to have everything prepared or reviewed by an attorney familiar with business sale transactions. This can avoid costly mistakes that can come back to haunt you later.

No matter which method of selling you choose, it is imperative that you fully understand the financial and legal issues of the sale and afterward. Your accountant should advise you regarding the financial statements of your company and the taxation matters that could result from the sale. Your attorney should advise on any legal issues that you do not fully understand in order to avoid any matters that may be overlooked and could incur legal liability for you during or after the transaction.

No matter which method of selling you choose, it is imperative that you do not misrepresent your company's past, present, or future in terms of income, expenses, and liabilities. Misrepresentation is a serious matter in courts of law, particularly in business sale transactions.

## Professional Representation

Representation by a professional will require execution of an agreement setting out the terms and conditions of the engagement. This could include the term of the agreement, the selling price agreed to, the duties of the professional and the seller, the obligation of the seller to pay a fee to the professional and the terms of such fee, the exclusiveness of the right to sell, and other important provisions.

If you enter into such an agreement, be sure you fully understand the terms. Most professionals in the business of selling businesses have the utmost integrity; however, as you are probably aware, you need to guard against the bad apples in the barrel. Don't be shy about asking for credentials and references when preparing to enter into an agreement to sell your company. The safest way to start is with professionals who belong to specialized organizations of brokers and intermediaries. The less safe way to start is with national organizations that advertise nationwide and have agents who roam big territories and charge large up-front fees.

The most often misleading come-on in soliciting engagements is the worn-out statement of "I have a buyer for your business" or "I am representing someone who wants to buy your company." These may be true but usually are not. They usually are ways of getting a meeting with you to convince you to sign up with them to sell your company, and the buyer they seemed to have in their pocket turns out to be mythological. Then you end up with an agreement for six months or a year or longer and sometimes are obligated to pay fees during the representation period.

Caution is recommended. When approached by solicitors of seller listings, ask what organizations they belong to. Ask what credentials and accreditations they have. If you are unconvinced of the qualifications and integrity, ask for references of companies previously represented. It often pays to shop around until you feel comfortable with one company or individual to represent you in this event, perhaps one of the most important events in your business life.

## A Case History: The Costs and Consequences of Misrepresentation

> A restaurant owner contacted me to discuss selling his restaurant that specialized in an ethnic type of food. The restaurant had been in business for many years. It was in an attractive, freestanding building at a very busy

thoroughfare in the city and had a good clientele. The business was listed at a price of $600,000. The owners had declared an income of $160,000 annually. A buyer who had been looking for a restaurant of this ethnicity came forward immediately after the restaurant was advertised. After some production of information, showing of the facilities, meetings with the owner, and purchase negotiations, an offer to purchase was presented to the seller, and a contract of sale was executed.

This began the due diligence period when the buyer observes the running of the business and studies, reviews documents and financial statements, and audits some of the historical reports of sales and expenses, all necessary to convince himself to go through with the acquisition. During this period, the buyer asked to review the daily reports for the restaurant for the last year. This prove-out of income transpired between the buyer and the seller exclusively, and the buyer reviewed all of the daily receipt reports for the entire year.

There were discussions and arguments about fixtures, musical systems, and décor that the seller desired not to be included in the sale. Finally, after all issues had presumably been resolved, an agreement was made, a final contract was signed, and escrow was opened. The final sale price was $550,000, all cash, at closing.

So the sale closed, the buyer took possession, and the seller received his money.

However, that was not the end of the story. A few months later, after the buyer had operated the restaurant for a while, he realized the payroll was much higher and the sales were somewhat less than he had been informed of. Apparently, the review of daily receipts had been requested because the seller had informed the buyer in private that the sales were greater than the income statement reflected. In other words, there was significant unreported income.

The buyer also realized that some of the kitchen equipment, which he had been informed was in good condition, had to be replaced and there were roof leak problems requiring repair that, under the lease provisions, were the tenant's responsibility. The buyer had been granted an inspection of the premises by a professional inspector. The seller had agreed to take care of any issues that were discovered.

The buyer soon initiated legal action against the seller for misrepresentation. The case lingered in the courts for a period of time and then was submitted to a mediator for a binding mediation. A mutually agreed judge was appointed to monitor the mediation. After several days of testimony of the parties involved and presentation of the seller's tax returns and other business records, it was decided that the seller did misrepresent the income and condition of the restaurant. The seller lost a large award to the buyer, including legal fees for the buyer. The seller ended up in much worse financial condition after paying the judgment to buyer and legal fees.

So do not misrepresent. Disclose, disclose, disclose. Do not misrepresent. Do not try to sell unreported income. And make sure that your attorney and financial advisor are consulted to answer and explain any part of the process that you do not fully understand, as well as the duty you owe to the buyer in your representation of the business.

# CHAPTER 9

## *Identifying a Potential Buyer*

### Buyer Sources

In marketing the company, you should first consider who the potential buyers might be. This depends somewhat on the size and type of your company. In the sale of a business, the buyer may come from a variety of sources.

- **A family member:** Family members are often the source for continuing a business operation, especially if the chosen family member has been involved in the management prior to the owner's decision to exit the business. This is often the owner's first choice. The disadvantage for the owner is lack of financing and unwillingness to foreclose if the company fails to succeed. If you sell your company to a child or other relative, will you be able to receive the sale price in the future? Will you be able to foreclose and resume control of the company if it doesn't go well? Chances are that you will not be willing to take these steps, which emphasizes the importance of fully analyzing the possibilities and probabilities in advance of making that decision. The wrong decision can affect personal as well as business relationships.

- **A person with committed funding:** Everyone's first choice, other than a family member, is someone with cash or funding to pay the purchase price. This eliminates the problem of the new owner failing and defaulting on any portion of the purchase price still owing to the previous owner. Business sale offerings seldom attract many well-funded inquirers, but they do exist. When such an inquiry comes about, it should receive your full attention.
- **A person with limited funds:** Limited funding is a common situation and should require full consideration of the funding ability of the buyer from outside sources without the seller carrying notes. Seller notes are a common element of funding but should usually be limited to a small portion of the sale price, if possible. It is important in this decision that you consider the damage that could occur and your ability to repossess the company and resume operations.
- **A person seeking a business in the industry:** A person looking for a business in your industry would be a favored choice if he or she has experience or knowledge of the industry. This would enhance the likeliness of outside funding and success in operation of the company. Such a buyer would also reduce the risks inherent in seller financing if it were required to fund the transaction.
- **An investor or investment group seeking a company in your industry:** An investor or investment group would generally be a desirable source for a buyer. There would usually be reliable funding sources and less of a requirement of seller financing, eliminating the fear of recourse or repossession.

- **A competitor seeking an acquisition:** Competitors can frequently be buyers and provide their own set of concerns. They can damage you in the process if they disappear after learning about your operations. They can damage you by attempting to pilfer off your customers or employees. Caution is the word when dealing with competitors. They often don't need your facilities or employees, but they really want your customers and your modus operandi. The likelihood of them paying your price is usually limited. Competitors generally don't need your facilities or all of your employees, but they are generally only interested in your customers.
- **An employee or group of employees:** An employee or group of employees can be a buyer source but can also create their own set of drawbacks. In order to fund the transaction, you often will be required to finance them personally with a seller note or guarantee their bank financing. Many employees can be great at what they do but are incapable of managing the company. In many cases, they fail, and the previous owner either has to repossess the company, forgo repayment of the seller note, or personally pay off the bank note guaranteed for the sale funding. Such a transaction deserves a great deal of scrutiny and assurance that the acquiring employees are capable of running the company and obtaining outside funding.
- **A potential immigrant through a visa program:** This can be a good source of a buyer, but I recommend not providing seller financing in this case. Typically, the visa program buyer has adequate funding and is not dependent upon the business to be successful in order for him or her to survive. The primary goal often is to immigrate into the country, and his

or her interest in operating the company can be minimal or nonexistent.

- **Baby boomers:** In today's environment, many so-called baby boomers are retired or semiretired. Some have financial means, and they are seeking good small businesses to acquire and build in order to provide additional income and something to occupy their time and minds. This source has been enlarged somewhat by the economic problems in the last several years, during which time investors lost significant value in their retirement funds and their cash savings came to receive little interest income.
- **A private equity group seeking a platform company:** Many private equity groups (PEGs) are looking for good, profitable companies to acquire and build for future disposition. These acquirers would typically be well funded and often would prefer that the seller stay on to run the company for a period of time, which sometimes works out well for the seller.
- **A PEG seeking add-on companies:** PEGs also are often seeking add-ons for platform companies they are building for future disposition. In this event, they sometimes will consider smaller companies that do not meet their size and profitability criteria for platform company acquisitions. Funding is rarely a problem in such transactions.

## PEGs

Most of the usual buyers listed above are of common knowledge to potential sellers of companies. The PEGs came into prominence a few decades ago and have grown rapidly as a source of business transfers, primarily for businesses of a size large enough to make a PEG's business plan work. Some PEGs like to buy companies, inject financial resources and management, promote growth through acquisition of similar companies, outsource and/or eliminate some segments, and sometimes just merge the acquisition into another company. They do whatever money or expertise can do to grow the company or make it more profitable. Then in a few years, they may sell the company or make an initial public offering (IPO) and convert it to a public company, thereby recovering their investment and earning a substantial profit on the deal.

PEGs are funded primarily by sources with significant cash to invest for long periods of time, such as colleges and university endowment funds, pension funds, hospital endowment funds, wealthy individuals, investment funds, hedge funds, and other sources with the capacity to take higher risks for higher returns on investment. The PEG receives funding commitments from eligible investors for a period of years and must invest the funds during such period or return whatever is not invested back to the source. So they are aggressively looking for opportunities that meet their investment criteria.

The PEG concept grew slowly over the years, but in periods when low interest rates adversely affected investment funds, such as the last couple of decades, the PEGs grew much faster. This became a popular source of higher returns on investment. Today, there are probably hundreds of such firms around the country and thousands around the world. They have absorbed a large portion of the acquisitions of middle-market-sized companies that are offered to market, particularly those that fit their criteria of financial capacity and growth potential.

PEGs are not usually a buyer source for smaller companies due to the small size, limited profitability and growth potential, and fragility of small businesses. The most active PEGs generally are seeking companies with annual revenues from $10 million up to $500 million and EBITDA of $2 million to $100 million depending upon the size of the fund. The most common priority profile published by various PEGs is a search for companies with a minimum of $2 million in EBITDA, diversified customer base, good management, barriers to entry, history of steady growth, expanding industry, and an owner desiring to stay on for a period of time. They generally specify industries and regions of interest. These are the criteria expressed to merger and acquisition intermediaries and business brokers, and they are the general parameters expressed by mail and verbally by those seeking acquisitions.

## A Company Meeting PEG Priorities

The type of company that most PEGs seek would be similar to the company illustrated in the following income statement.

> I was engaged as a consultant in the decision-making process of selling this company. The ultimate disposition was a sale to the general manager of the company, along with an investment group. The seller stayed on in consultation and received substantial cash for retirement. He also personally owned the two industrial buildings the company occupied and, in turn, leased them to the company.
>
> This company had been in business for many years. They were a leader in their particular product line. They were financially healthy, stable, and free of debt, so they could

be leveraged up with new debt to fund new acquisitions for growth and provide up-front management fees for PEG principals.

Note that this company reflects sales of $14 million, healthy gross profit margins of greater than 40 percent, and net income of greater than 10 percent. The EBITDA, the description of earnings that PEGs most often use, was greater than 12 percent. These income features indicate good management and growth potential. The history of profitability and the status of being the industry leader supported the perceived strength required to sustain unfavorable business cycles.

**Ventilation Equipment Mfg Co.**
**P&L Comparisons**
**Periods 2003–2004**

| | 2003 | 2004 |
|---|---|---|
| **Total Sales** | 14,553,056 | 14,053,364 |
| Cost of goods sold | 8,163,713 | 8,184,459 |
| **Gross Profit** | 6,389,343 | 5,868,905 |
| | | |
| **Selling Expenses** | 1,977,033 | 1,901,520 |
| | | |
| **General & Administrative Expenses** | 2,763,693 | 2,624,084 |
| | | |
| **Operating Income** | 1,648,617 | 1,343,301 |
| Other income (expense) | 54,331 | 96,201 |
| **Net Income** | **1,702,948** | **1,439,502** |
| **Adjustments:** | | |
| Amortization | 82,054 | 82,054 |
| Depreciation | 95,063 | 66,222 |
| Officer salary adjust to market | 250,000 | 250,000 |
| Other income | (54,331) | (96,201) |
| **Total Adjustments** | **481,448** | **302,075** |
| | | |
| **EBITDA** | 2,184,396 | 1,741,577 |

Although they were on the smaller end of the financial scale preferred for such investments, their financial health, reputation, and potential growth increased the value of the company beyond a normal low multiple of earnings, which would be more common for smaller and more fragile companies. These factors made the deal work out well for the seller and enabled him to provide the ownership opportunity for his valued employee.

## A Company Not Meeting PEG Priorities

This company manufactures jewelry from raw materials such as gold, silver, and other materials. They provide a complete line of exclusive, proprietary designs of many types of jewelry. PEG firms would typically not seek after the company featured in the illustration below:

**Jewelry Manufacturing Co**
**P&L Comparisons**
**2002–2004**

| | 2002 | 2003 | 2004 |
|---|---|---|---|
| **Sales** | 8,749,051 | 10,003,293 | 8,649,606 |
| Cost of goods sold | 7,378,661 | 8,706,518 | 7,685,613 |
| **Gross Profit** | 1,370,390 | 1,296,775 | 963,993 |
| Profit margin | 16 percent | 13 percent | 11 percent |
| **Total Expenses** | 1,369,495 | 1,274,994 | 1,257,067 |
| **Net Income before Taxes** | 895 | 21,781 | -293,074 |
| **Adjustments** | | | |
| Amortization | 177,869 | 151,959 | 139,238 |
| Depreciation | 136,983 | 218,708 | 110,962 |
| Interest expense | 238,036 | 258,754 | 284,233 |
| Officer salary adjust to mkt | -250,000 | (250,000 | (250,000 |
| **Total Adjustments** | 302,888 | 379,421 | 284,433 |
| | | | |
| **EBITDA** | **303,783** | **401,202** | **-8,641** |

Note the profit margins on sales, which are dangerously low for a manufacturer, particularly in a market of fluctuating values of precious metals. Profit margins of manufacturing in general are typically 35 percent or greater; otherwise, there isn't a sufficient gross profit to cover sales and administrative costs and the expenses of facilities and legal aspects of the operations. This company's gross profit margin of 11 to 16 percent is usually the desirable minimal bottom line of net profit sought, which would indicate a company with sustainable income and growth potential. A profit margin such as this company reflects indicates a fragile condition with little room to sustain downturns in revenues or increases in costs of operations.

Note that operating expenses are equivalent to or greater than profit margins, as was discussed above as inadequate profit margin to cover operating expenses.

Note that there is little or no net income in 2002 and 2003 and a loss of nearly $300,000 in 2004. By adjusting the statement for EBITDA, it reflects figures of $300,000 in 2002, $400,000 in 2003, and a negative in 2004.

A husband and wife both work full time in management of the company; therefore, officer salary was adjusted upward to reflect the value of unpaid salary that would have to be replaced with a new owner. This company operates in a very cyclical industry directly affected by fluctuations in discretionary spending and is the first and hardest industry usually affected in an economic downturn. They finance their largest cost in raw materials, which is gold, through a gold leasing program. Every fluctuation in gold prices has a direct effect on the value of their inventory and cost structure. The thin profit margin under which they operate is insufficient to withstand these volatile fluctuations. As a supplier for smaller independent jewelry retailers, they must compete with the larger retail jewelers, many of whom have their own manufacturing sources in cheaper labor markets. This type of company would generally not interest a PEG, even though they have adequate size, due to the fragility and instability of their niche in the market.

The above income statement was abbreviated for illustration purposes. The entire statement is shown below:

| Jewelry Manufacturing Co.<br>P&L Comparisons<br>2002–2004 | | | |
|---|---|---|---|
| | 2002 | 2003 | 2004 |
| **Sales** | 8,749,051 | 10,003,293 | 8,649,606 |
| Cost of goods sold | 7,378,661 | 8,706,518 | 7,685,613 |
| **Gross Profit** | 1,370,390 | 1,296,775 | 963,993 |
| Profit margin | 16 percent | 13 percent | 11 percent |
| | | | |
| **Expenses** | | | |
| Advertising | 49,940 | 37,747 | 40,188 |
| Amortization | 177,869 | 151,959 | 139,238 |
| Automobile | 10,094 | 6,157 | 8,572 |
| Bad debts | 103,070 | | |
| Bank charges | 15,167 | 37,114 | 17,730 |
| Charitable contributions | 2,148 | 1,100 | |
| Commission | 5,332 | 13,102 | 42,192 |
| Depreciation | 37,871 | 60,774 | 29,629 |
| Dues and subscriptions | 4,862 | 5,367 | 6,506 |
| Equipment rental | 24,694 | 19,582 | 10,773 |
| Insurance | 41,581 | 48,633 | 54,936 |
| Insurance-Workers Comp. | 5,355 | 11,359 | |
| Interest expense | 238,036 | 258,754 | 284,233 |
| Legal and professional | 49,312 | 25,675 | 68,619 |
| Office expense | 27,105 | 10,505 | 18,624 |
| Postage | 9,504 | 13,066 | 21,721 |
| Rent | 48,000 | 48,000 | 51,200 |
| Repairs and maintenance | 12,873 | 10,679 | 9,307 |

| | | | | |
|---|---|---|---|---|
| | Salaries and wages | 254,484 | 290,091 | 246,427 |
| | Salaries-Officers | 73,360 | 73,360 | 73,360 |
| | Security | 10,355 | 5,121 | 4,719 |
| | Supplies | 27,492 | 16,336 | |
| | Taxes and licenses | 62,298 | 71,597 | 76,217 |
| | Telephone | 17,340 | 17,315 | 18,055 |
| | Trade shows and promotion | 24,296 | | |
| | Travel and entertainment | 13,755 | 20,665 | 13,108 |
| | Utilities | 23,302 | 20,936 | 21,713 |
| **Total Expenses** | | 1,369,495 | 1,274,994 | 1,257,067 |
| **Net Income before Taxes** | | 895 | 21,781 | (293,074) |
| **Adjustments:** | | | | |
| | Amortization | 177,869 | 151,959 | 139,238 |
| | Depreciation | 136,983 | 218,708 | 110,962 |
| | Interest expense | 238,036 | 258,754 | 284,233 |
| | Officer salary adjust to mkt | (250,000) | (250,000 | (250,000 |
| **Total Adjustments** | | 302,888 | 379,421 | 284,433 |
| **EBITDA** | | 303,783 | 401,202 | (8,641) |

## Some PEG Practices Worth Noting

Some firms in this PEG market have become known by the practice of buying companies with borrowing capacity, loading them up with new debt, pulling sizable fees out for the principals of the PEG firm, selling off divisions, and, if performance doesn't go so well, sometimes putting the company into bankruptcy protection, thereby positioning themselves to run the firm during the bankruptcy and earning significant management fees during the process. Fortunately, most PEGs do not operate in such a way but have the utmost integrity. If your company is the size that fits into the priorities sought by these firms, you can often realize a rewarding sale of your company, but caution should be used in interviewing and getting under contract with them until you have determined their history and mode of operation and carefully considered the ultimate outcome of the process.

There are those PEGs seeking smaller companies for add-ons for a platform company they are trying to grow. In those cases, a company with smaller annual revenue and lesser profitability could be a good source for them. This can also be a rewarding opportunity for the disposition of your company.

# CHAPTER 10

## *Ways of Marketing Your Company for Sale*

Marketing the company can be done in many different ways depending upon the urgency of a sale, the level of confidentiality required, the type of business, and the size of the company. This phase of the business sale process has changed more than any other with the advent of the Internet. With the Internet, we can now get any information we want out as fast and as far as we desire as long as we have the capacity to post the offerings properly and attract attention through Internet expertise, such as search engine optimization (SEO) of your website or other sites utilized.

- **Websites:** Many business sale websites can be used for advertising a business for sale. Some of these sites allow postings for free, some charge a monthly or one-time fee, and some allow priority exposure for an additional fee. Some can be consulted regarding advertising (www.IBBA.org, www.bizben.com, www.businessbrokers.net, www.businessforsale.com, www.bizquest.com, and www.loopnet.com). And there are several others. Just query your favorite search engine for such sites, and you will get various suggestions. You can establish a single-purpose website just to advertise your business and then use an e-mail campaign to attract hits from potential interested parties. This can be done through some website hosting companies by the subscriber, or it can be done by hiring the hosting company to do all the work.

- **E-mail campaigns:** E-mail campaigns can be used to attract interested parties by utilizing e-mail lists available from companies assembling such lists. You can purchase an e-mail list of companies in your industry, if one is available, and send periodic e-mails to those potential acquirers.
- **Direct mail:** You can send direct mail pieces to potential interested parties with a blind flyer describing the company without divulging the name of the company.
- **Trade publications:** You can advertise in trade publications of the industry you are targeting or in local or national newspapers, such as the *Wall Street Journal.* With the overwhelming success of the Internet, newspaper advertising is not utilized as often as it once was; however, most publications include Internet editions in addition to their print editions, so you can get better results from a given industry with this source.
- **The brokerage industry:** You can offer your company for sale to most of the business brokers in the country through the broker industry organizations. The websites for these organizations list their members with contact information. If some brokers have a client seeking an acquisition in your industry and area, a match may work for you.

The most appropriate and worthwhile method of advertising for your buyer may be through a company that can build a simple website to describe your company and then do some professional SEO campaigns to promote the site. These are done with key words and other procedures to attract those seeking your type of company or opportunity. This can be promoted further with a targeted e-mail campaign to potential parties of interest with a referral to your specific website.

## Engaging Professional Marketing Organizations

If you choose to engage a professional organization to represent you during the sale process, you can find many possible sources through industry organizations, such as

- International Business Brokers Association (www.IBBA.org), 3525 Piedmont Road NE, Building 5, Suite 300, Atlanta, GA 30305, Phone: 888.686.IBBA (4222), Fax: 404.240.0998
- Merger & Acquisition Source (www.IBBA.org), 3525 Piedmont Road NE, Building 5, Suite 300, Atlanta, GA 30305, Phone: 404.477.5810, Fax: 404.240.0998
- Association for Corporate Growth, ACG Global Headquarters, 125 S. Wacker Drive, Suite 3100, Chicago, IL 60606, Phone: 877.358.2220

## Other National and State Organizations

For state or local organizations, use your favorite search engine and query for business broker or merger and acquisition organizations in your area. These organizations provide training, education, and certification verifying the education and skill level of those accredited with their professional designations. They provide their members with the current tools, resources, and knowledge to represent and market companies in compliance with state and federal laws and the organization's standards of conduct.

Representatives of these organizations, as well as brokers not aligned therewith, generally charge 10 percent or more of the sale price of a small business as a success fee upon a successful sale transaction. Often, they charge up-front fees to cover the costs of preparation, valuation, and advertising. In the case of larger businesses, the fee percentage sometimes is scaled at lower rates for different enterprise sale values, and up-front fees and progress payments during the sale process may be greater. Each possible representative organization will have its own set of fees and charges.

## Potential Pitfalls in Marketing Your Company

Most of the many practitioners in the business of selling businesses are legitimate and operate with complete integrity and professionalism. That especially includes those who affiliate with the IBBA, M&A Source, and similar organizations. These organizations generally have codes of ethics to which the members must adhere. However, as in most any industry, there are some bad apples in the barrel.

A few years ago, a company in California maintained a continuous national advertising campaign to attract business owners to an inexpensive seminar to learn how to sell their business for big money. Some business owners reported receiving such invitations on a weekly or monthly basis, year after year. Attendees were asked to pay a fee of a hundred dollars or so and attend a one-day seminar in their local area.

The company would send one of their speakers to a town to conduct a seminar. They would walk people through all the various stages of selling their businesses, explaining the ways in which they could show an attractive value of the company. At the end of the day, they would attempt to convince attendees to engage the company to do a valuation and pricing study of their company. The cost of this engagement was $30,000 to $50,000 and took several weeks. After they completed their analysis, they would prepare a leather-bound book with all of the financial data and other information they had compiled about the company, along with their opinion of value. This book would include fifty or so pages of graphs, charts, financial calculations, and descriptive dialog about the features of the company.

They would then attempt to convince the company owner to engage them to sell the company, which would require them to pay a sizable up-front fee to do the preparation and advertising and then a success fee at such time as they sold the company.

As one could imagine, there were many more seminar fees than valuation fees, there were many more valuation fees than up-front fees, and there were many more up-front fees than success fees. So this company became known to live off seminar, valuation, and up-front fees.

This analysis of aggressive marketing organizations is merely intended to caution you in dealing with those with stories and promises that seem too good to be true. They can be very costly and do much damage without producing any results.

## Case History: Beware of Fraudulent Valuations

The following case explains the importance of the advice, "Don't believe everything you hear."

> There was a furniture store in a touristy California city whose owner wanted to sell out and retire. The store was well founded in the area and produced a good income, and

it was doing several million dollars in annual sales. The storeowner contacted me, as a business advisor, to meet and discuss the possibility of selling the enterprise. I agreed to do a quick study of the financials and operations and provide an opinion of value for the enterprise.

After analyzing the data provided, I informed the furniture storeowner that, although the store had good earnings and growth, the industry was quite cyclical and the store carried a very high inventory value, which increased the total investment for a buyer substantially. I felt it would probably not support more than 3 times multiple of earnings. I projected the business to sell for a price of $1 to $1.2 million.

The owner had been to a seminar of a valuation-offering company. The principal of this company, upon realization that they may have a live one, made a special trip to see this owner, briefly reviewed his financial statements and operations, and told him that the store would sell for at least $4 to $5 million guaranteed! With that good news, the owner then agreed to pay this company a fee of $43,000 to do a complete valuation and review of the company. This took about two months, at which time the owner was presented with a hardbound book about his company with comprehensive explanations of all calculations and data used in the review. The conclusion placed a value of $1 to $1.5 million on the company, with a final suggested selling price of $1.2 million.

> Upon receipt of this disappointing information, the furious owner contacted his attorney immediately, claiming he had been misled or defrauded. After a short period of threats against the valuation company, they agreed to refund half of the fee they had collected from the business owner by expressing an opinion of value of his company, which was absurd at best.
>
> The elapsed time and changing economy during this time left the seller disenchanted and in a weaker financial position. The result was the hiring of a company specializing in extended closeout sales. The business was then liquidated in sixty days.

The lesson from this case is to be careful who and what you believe when it comes to selecting someone to offer your company to market. You may be led astray. In other words, don't believe everything you hear.

# CHAPTER 11

## *Providing Information Necessary for a Sale*

The process of offering a business for sale involves a number of steps that are important in order to provide the information that a potential buyer would need to determine the feasibility of an acquisition. These steps are essential, whether a professional in the business sale industry makes the offering or the owner puts up the company for sale.

### Prepare Information in Advance

The realization that the potential buyer could come from such differing sources and have such various criteria of selection emphasizes the need for comprehensive information to be prepared to comply with various requests. Without advance preparation of marketing information about the company, the time required for preparing information for various requests could delay the response and cause loss of interest on the part of inquirers, so preparation in advance can be very important. Like industry veterans say, "Time kills all deals."

## Comprehensive Information

Comprehensive information must provide interested parties a description of the company, the products or services, the facilities, the staff, the ownership, the management, the organizational structure, the financial structure, the profit and loss statements, balance sheets, income statements, and other financial and organizational data. The information should be historical, current, and projected. The interested party needs to know where the company has been, where it is now, and where it is going or could go in the future. The information should be accurate and verifiable without claims and projections that seem unrealistic or beyond expectations.

## Project Integrity and Completeness

If an interested party gets the feeling that an offering has been misrepresented, the awareness diminishes interest rapidly, and further information is not given full value. It generates the fear of dishonesty and creates a tendency to disbelieve or question any additional features emphasized about the company. This can have a negative effect on the valuation and desirability of the company and becomes a deterrent to finding a ready, willing, and able buyer.

## Focus on the Inherent Value, Not Blue Sky

If the focus of the value of the company is entirely on what the buyer could do with the company to make it more valuable or profitable, the general thought for the potential buyer would typically be, "Why didn't the present owner do those steps and make it more successful?" If there is an inference of greater value by changing courses, adding products, or approaching other customers, the neglect of the current owner taking those actions must have a simple and believable explanation, and the likelihood of success from such actions must be considered reasonably certain to be successful.

I have heard many claims of greater potential for a given company from sellers, such as adding larger facilities, different equipment, more specialized employees, or better salespeople; taking on new product lines; expanding into other territories or other states; cutting expenses; or dropping lines of product or divisions of the operation. All is maybe true or possible, but the potential buyer can really only see what is on the seller's financial statements and would be inclined to believe that, if such actions were so readily available to increase sales and profits, that the seller would have already taken such actions. This is sometimes called fluff. It is hard to sell fluff.

The buyer is inclined to assess the company's value by what the seller has accomplished, not by what can be done. If the buyer believes that the business can be grown, then that element has already been added into the calculation. The buyer does not want to pay for potential growth. If the company grows in the future, the buyer expects that to be his or her reward for diligence and ingenuity.

## Encourage Confidentiality

Once conversation between the owner and the interested buyer ensues, the company owner can make a determination regarding the advisability of providing additional information about the company. If the decision is made to provide additional information, it is usually advisable to obtain a nondisclosure agreement in writing from the interested party prior to divulging any information that could be damaging to the company in any way. This is a good deterrent to information about the company getting into the wrong hands and being used adversely against the company.

Confidentiality of information about the sale and information about your company is always an important consideration as the company is advertised to attract interested parties, you meet with interested parties, volumes of information are provided, negotiations transpire, offers are considered, and escrow is accomplished. Of course, the sale can break down at any one of these points and frequently does. The lasting effect is the exposure of the confidential knowledge about the sale and proprietary information about the company's operations to employees, customers, vendors, bankers, and other investors.

Some employees, should they gain knowledge of a potential sale, could seek other opportunities in order to assure their own livelihood in the event of a change of ownership that they disapproved of or in the event that the new ownership did not wish to retain their services.

An unscrupulous competitor could use the information to damage the company with current or potential customers by simply dropping the word that the company is being sold. The current owner may never know that it happened and therefore not know why the competitor gained favor with their customer or potential purchaser.

The same competitor may be able to hire away some of the company's key employees without the current owner realizing it in advance and therefore not making any effort of retention. The same competitor also may wish to gain knowledge of a product, process, business practice, or relationship that the company has created and thereby gain a lead in order to reduce the company's advantage in the market or industry.

You, as the seller, must be fully aware of the risk of a breach of confidentiality and the damages it could cause. It is best to consider all of the possibilities in advance and take steps to guard against potential harm and advise critical relationships or parties of the company's plans as much as possible. You should be fully aware that the likelihood of retaining confidentiality reduces more and more the longer the company is on the market.

The following is an example of a nondisclosure agreement that can be obtained from an interested party in order to limit exposure of the company information and knowledge of intent to sell the company. The format of legal content will vary with practitioners in the industry, but the importance centers on deterrence of a breach of the nondisclosure agreement.

## CONFIDENTIALITY AND NONDISCLOSURE AGREEMENT

The undersigned, individually and on behalf of any affiliated prospective buyer, requests information relating to the following business: **located in ______________________ ("Business")**. Such information shall be provided to the undersigned for the sole purpose of entering into discussions with Seller ("Seller") of said Business for the possible purchase by the undersigned of all or part of the stock or assets of Business. As used herein, the term Buyer ("Buyer") applies to the undersigned and any partnership, corporation, individual, or other entity with which the undersigned is affiliated. The undersigned agrees as follows:

1. **NONDISCLOSURE of INFORMATION:** The undersigned acknowledges that Seller desires to maintain the confidentiality of the information disclosed. The undersigned agrees with Broker not to disclose or permit access to any

Confidential Information without the prior written consent of Seller to anyone other than Buyer's employees, legal counsel, accountants, lenders, or other agents or advisors to whom disclosure or access is necessary for Buyer to evaluate the Business. Disclosure of Confidential Information shall be made to these parties only in connection with the potential acquisition of the Business and then only if these parties understand and agree to maintain the confidentiality of such Confidential Information. The undersigned shall be responsible for any breach of this Agreement by these parties, and neither Buyer nor these parties shall use or permit the use of Confidential Information in any manner whatsoever, except as may be required for Buyer to evaluate the Business or as may be required for legal process. If Buyer does not purchase the Business, Buyer, at the close of negotiations, will destroy or return to Broker (at Broker's option) all information provided to Buyer and will not retain any copy, reproduction, or record thereof.

2. **DEFINITION of CONFIDENTIAL INFORMATION:** The term Confidential Information shall mean all information, including the fact that the Business is for sale; all financial, production, marketing, and pricing information; business methods; business manuals; manufacturing procedures; correspondence; processes; contracts; customer lists; employee lists; and any other information, whether written, oral, or otherwise made known to Buyer: (a) from any inspection, examination, or other review of the books, records, assets, liabilities, processes, or production methods of Seller; (b) from communications with Seller or its directors, officers, employees, agents, suppliers, customers,

or representatives; (c) during visits to Seller's premises, or (d) through disclosure or discovery in any other manner. However, Confidential Information does not include any information that is readily available and known to the public.

3. **FURTHER TERMS:** Neither Buyer nor Buyer's agent will contact Seller's employees, customers, landlords, or suppliers without Seller's consent. For three years, Buyer shall not directly or indirectly solicit for employment any employees of Seller. Broker may act as a dual agent representing both Buyer and Seller. Seller is specifically intended to be a beneficiary of the duties and obligations of the Agreement and may prosecute any action at law or in equity necessary to enforce its terms and conditions as though a party hereto. Seller may assign this Agreement to any new ownership of Business. This agreement can only be modified in writing, signed by both Broker and Buyer. Waiver of any breach of this Agreement shall not be a waiver of any subsequent breach. This Agreement supersedes all prior understandings or agreements between the parties with respect to its subject matter. If Buyer is a corporation, partnership, or other such entity, the undersigned executes this Agreement on behalf of Buyer and warrants that he or she is duly authorized to do so. **Buyer acknowledges receipt of a copy of this Agreement.**

By__________________ By __________________

**Information submitted by the buyer**

## Buyer's Experience Qualifications

All businesses and all industries do not require similar education, knowledge, or experience in order to be managed effectively. However, most all businesses require some business and management skills, and some require technical knowledge to operate effectively. Some require educational requirements for licensing and certification in order to operate the business. The importance at this stage is to determine if an interested party has a background, education, or experience necessary to understand and effectively manage the business at hand.

Such a consideration is important in order to limit exposure of liability to a buyer if a business fails after a transfer of ownership. Liability for the buyer's failure is often not a consideration for sellers of companies, but it should be. Too many business sale transactions end up in litigation after the buyer fails and accuses the seller of misrepresentation. Although this is usually not the case, it can burden the seller with time and money-consuming litigation and destroy the reward gained from what the seller thought was a good disposition of the company.

If the company being offered for sale is a manufacturing company, the future owner or manager should have some background in manufacturing, engineering, or some related industry requiring an understanding of mechanical machinery and manufacturing processes. Even if manufacturing is outsourced, the owner should understand the processes, materials, and design features in order to outsource intelligently and assure quality control. Selling defective or poorly designed products can lead to early failure for most any industry.

If the company being offered is involved in food service, which is the case in many small business transactions, the buyer should have some background in food preparation or service, not only in terms of understanding the fine details of the business but in comprehending the difficulties and risks involved. One question often asked of those interested in acquiring small restaurant operations is: What do you know about cooking, purchasing food products, and serving food? The reason being, that if the cook, server, or manager doesn't show up, the new owner may be doing his or her job. And if the new owner doesn't understand the job, it will be difficult to teach a new employee how best to perform the duties. It certainly isn't prudent to close the café because the cook didn't show up. The reason this is critical in the restaurant business is that the owner only gets one chance to impress a customer with good food and service. If he fails, he usually won't see him or her again.

If the company being offered for sale requires some type of special knowledge, certification, or credentials to obtain licensing, certification, or governmental approval to operate, then the seller should be assured that the potential buyer could accomplish the requirements. Otherwise, the time and effort is wasted, and confidentiality is unnecessarily exposed. For instance, a company manufacturing or selling pharmaceutical products will probably require an FDA license and will be monitored and inspected by the FDA. This may require certain members of the staff to have educational degrees in pharmacy, chemistry, medicine, or other critical sciences. Without such capability, the company could not operate in the industry. The seller should have some assurance early in the discussions of the ability of the buyer to fulfill that requirement.

If there is a franchise, dealership, or vendor approval required to operate the company, the seller should have some assurance that the buyer can qualify for such approval, or the company may not be granted necessary approval or cannot continue to function.

## Buyer's Financial Qualifications

Many business sale transactions fail because of the buyer's inability to finance the acquisition. The seller should determine a buyer's financial condition prior to entering into advanced discussions involving proprietary information about the company. The seller should give priority to potential buyers who have verified an adequate source of funds to complete the transaction. The reasons are many, but the primary reasons are time and confidentiality. Spending time with an unqualified buyer often causes a seller to miss better opportunities because of the belief that the unqualified party can perform without verifiable capital. Implications, such as "my investors" or "I have investors," often imply sources of capital that do not exist except in the hopes of buyers. Never put trust in the promise of investors unless their involvement is verifiable. The investors often do not exist, and if they do, they often get cold feet before the closing of the deal. If the acquisition is to be acquired through investors, the funds should be proven and verified for that use. Otherwise, time and confidentiality is again wasted. It doesn't make much sense to expose confidentiality of proprietary information that could damage the company or the fact that the company is on the market unless the seller is dealing with a qualified buyer.

The following is an example of a form for buyer information:

# ACQUISITION QUESTIONNAIRE

This questionnaire is for the registration of interest in acquiring a business. All information herein is confidential and is for distribution to owners of, or the legal or financial advisors of, companies of interest of the undersigned. __________ representatives are hereby authorized to submit this information as they deem necessary for the purpose above stated.

| *General Information* | | | |
|---|---|---|---|
| Name | Company | | Position |
| Address | City | State | Zip Code |
| Home Phone | Work Phone | E-mail | |
| Business of Interest: | | | |
| Business Currently Owned: | Name: | Address: | |
| How Long in Business: | Annual Revenue: | Annual Earnings: | |
| Business or Employment Background: | | | |
| | | | |

| *Please List Only the Funds that you would use for a Business Acquisition* | | |
|---|---|---|
| Type of funds available | Amount of funds available | Date funds will be available or explanation |
| Cash | $ | |
| Stocks & Bonds | $ | |
| Notes Receivable | $ | |
| Real Estate Equity | $ | |
| Other Investors | $ | |
| | $ | |
| Total Funds Available for Acquisition | $ | |

| *Time Frame* | |
|---|---|
| Are you ready to purchase a business now? If no, when? | |
| *Comments* | |
| | |
| | |
| **Signature** | **Date** |

## Information Submitted by Seller

### The Blind Flyer

The professional approach to marketing normally initiates with a one- or two-page flyer with general information about the company. This is sometimes referred to as a blind flyer, as it would not reveal the name or location of the company or information that would identify the company to a competitor, employee, or customer. The importance of this is confidentiality. The offering should be done in such a way as to limit the possibility of collateral damage by competitors disclosing your intent to sell your company to your customers or employees. Customers could become concerned with the availability of the company's products or services and employees could become concerned with their careers or job security.

The following provides an example of a simple one- or two-page blind flyer that could be used as a brief description of a company's products and services. This piece should be explanatory but confidential. It should give the interested party a quick indication of whether the company is of any additional interest to him or her and if further information is necessary to determine if the opportunity may be advantageous or feasible.

**Chemical Laboratory & Manufacturing Company**

**Formulation, Manufacturing, Private Labeling**

**Cosmetics—Skin Care—Hair Care—Pharmaceuticals**

**This chemical laboratory, manufacturing and packaging company was founded in 1970.** In its thirty-eight years of existence, the company has earned a reputation as a leading company in manufacturing, packaging, and private labeling of liquids, creams, and lotions for the pharmaceutical, cosmetic, and specialty products industries. The company specializes in product formulation, compounding, filling, and packaging of skin care and hair care products, over-the-counter drug items, health and nutritional supplements, health drinks, and ethnic skin and hair care products.

**Located in Chicago, Illinois**, the company employs more than sixty thoroughly trained and highly skilled staff. The offices, laboratory, and production facilities occupy a sixty-thousand-square-foot flexible manufacturing and warehousing building, equipped with fully automated state-of-the-art machinery. The facilities include a fully staffed analytical and research and development department and a microbiological laboratory.

**The company has produced thousands of formulations for many well-known firms.** Many products have ingredients and specifications that include essential oils of aromatherapy, aloe vera, and alpha hydroxy acid. They produce customer formulations, reformulate existing products, and create or develop new formulations.

**The company is licensed by the following federal, state, and city regulatory agencies:**

- US Food and Drug Administration (FDA)
- State Department of Health Services
- Environmental Protection Agency (EPA)
- Bureau of Alcohol, Tobacco, and Firearms

This contract product design and manufacturing company produces unexcelled, high quality products for its customers. The facilities are well equipped, well organized, and managed by a highly trained and competent staff. Barriers of entry in this industry are significant due to the difficulty in achieving the required customer confidence in producing high-quality products under precise quality control.

This company should be attractive to

1. potential acquirers in related industries in order to expand capabilities and
2. individual investors seeking a company with significant barriers of entry and growth potential.

Contact Information

**1234 Main Street, Anywhere, NY 10000**

**212-111-1111 – info@anywhere.com**

---

## Confidential Review

As interest in the company and the potential buyer progresses, additional information is usually required in order to move the interest to the next level. The owner should receive information about the potential buyer's ability to finance an acquisition and manage the company going forward. The potential buyer should receive comprehensive information about the company in order to evaluate it and determine if there is a good fit and future for the company.

Such additional information is often provided in a comprehensive study of the company, sometimes referred to as a confidential review. This thorough profile about the company would typically include these items:

- a listing and explanation of the company's products and services
- complete history from the company's inception to present
- description of the industry in which the company operates
- historical and current income statements, balance sheets, and cash flow statements
- projections of current year and following year's income
- description of the owners, management, and staff; the products or services provided; and the facilities and equipment
- future projections of the economy
- status and future projections of the industry
- photographs of company facilities, company products, and services
- summary of the features and value enhancers
- indication of potential interested parties

All of this information is important for the buyer to determine the financial feasibility of an acquisition, to see if the acquisition is a good fit personally, and to become comfortable with the historical success and future prospects for the company.

This proprietary information, which could be damaging to the seller, should not be revealed without the seller first determining the buyer's capability to make the acquisition and to finance the transaction.

Once the information is disclosed to a potential buyer, the seller has no control over where the information goes from there. The following people may review it: other employees of the buyer, family members, potential investors, lenders considering financing the transaction, appraisers, legal and financial advisors, or any others of interest in the acquisition or the seller's operations.

I am sure there are many stories concerning unscrupulous potential buyers of companies who either had no intention of acquiring the company or were unable to complete the transaction for some reason and then proceeded to siphon off the seller's customers or employees or used the opportunity for industrial espionage by stealing trade secrets, intellectual property, or processes used successfully by seller in developing the company into a leading company in the field or area.

These unfortunate outcomes can be avoided by following precautionary steps in the process of selling. Make sure you understand and feel comfortable with any potential buyer, and make sure he or she is ready, willing, and able. This includes being financially able. And don't divulge any information that can damage you except as contingencies of the sale after contracts are executed and financial capability is confirmed. It is sometimes necessary to require a walkaway fee, a nonrefundable deposit, or a penalty provision in the event of interference with or solicitation of your employees or customers for a specific period of time.

## Examples of Financial Records

The following examples provide some examples of financial records that would generally be essential for a potential buyer's examination and due diligence of the company in determining the feasibility of an acquisition.

## Income Statement

| Chemical Company<br>Profit / (Loss)<br>2007–2010 | | | | |
|---|---|---|---|---|
| **Period** | **2007** | **2008** | **2009** | **2010** |
| **Sales** | **7,776,229** | **6,631,600** | **6,042,626** | **7,525,372** |
| Cost of goods sold | 5,143,823 | 4,432,789 | 3,949,355 | 4,922,734 |
| **Gross Profit** | **2,632,406** | **2,198,811** | **2,093,271** | **2,602,638** |
| Total operating expenses | 2,467,330 | 2,345,235 | 2,377,569 | 2,345,629 |
| **Net Operating Income** | **165,076** | **(146,424)** | **(284,298)** | **257,009** |
| Other income | 18,471 | 13,264 | 12,594 | |
| Less interest expense | (154,162) | (125,424) | (92,986) | |
| **Net Income before Taxes** | **24,178** | **(259,254)** | **(370,284)** | **168,955** |
| Interest expense | 154,162 | 125,424 | 92,986 | 88,054 |
| Other income | (13,264) | (12,594) | (7,000) | |
| Depreciation | 119,469 | 100,612 | 93,675 | 70,147 |
| Other financial exp. | 1,875 | 4,900 | 12,022 | 14,141 |
| Extraordinary legal | | | | 40,000 |
| State franchise tax | 800 | 800 | 800 | 800 |
| **Total Adjustments** | **263,042** | **219,142** | **192,483** | **213,142** |
| **EBITDA** | **287,220** | **(40,112)** | **(177,801)** | **382,097** |

## Balance Sheet

| ABC Manufacturing Co., Inc. Balance Sheet | | | | |
|---|---|---|---|---|
| Year ending 12/31 | 2007 | 2008 | 2009 | 2010 |
| **ASSETS** | | | | |
| Cash | 38,217 | 19,977 | 34,113 | 20,341 |
| Accounts receivable | 1,133,733 | 936,105 | 705,629 | 502,589 |
| Inventory | 2,168,157 | 2,372,064 | 2,268,797 | 1,965,208 |
| Loan receivable | 252,162 | 68,347 | 386,692 | 511,088 |
| Due from fire loss claim | | 14,031 | | |
| Other current assets | 74,588 | 45,782 | 53,285 | 45,839 |
| **Total Current Assets** | **3,666,857** | **3,456,306** | **3,448,516** | **3,045,065** |
| Buildings and other fixed assets | 2,617,980 | 2,703,705 | 2,711,008 | 2,716,284 |
| Accumulated depreciation | (2,090,111) | (2,190,723) | (2,284,398) | (2,363,039) |
| **Total Fixed Assets** | **527,869** | **512,982** | **426,610** | **353,245** |
| Other assets | | | | 53,435 |
| **Total Assets** | **4,194,726** | **3,969,288** | **3,875,126** | **3,451,745** |
| | | | | |
| **LIABILITIES & EQUITY** | | | | |
| Accounts payable | 829,534 | 978,769 | 1,012,964 | 547,617 |
| Notes payable | 337,255 | 314,870 | 590,651 | |
| Other liabilities | 90,694 | 151,378 | 380,535 | 377,605 |
| **Total Current Liabilities** | **1,257,483** | **1,445,017** | **1,984,150** | **925,222** |
| Loans from shareholders | 109,957 | 141,583 | 106,657 | 126,415 |
| Notes payable | 1,451,826 | 1,266,482 | 1,053,595 | 1,499,430 |
| **Total Long-Term Liabilities** | **1,561,783** | **1,408,065** | **1,160,252** | **1,625,845** |
| Capital stock | 100,000 | 100,000 | 100,000 | 100,000 |
| Additional paid-in capital | 205,330 | 205,330 | 205,330 | 205,330 |
| Retained earnings | 1,070,130 | 810,876 | 425,394 | 694,348 |
| **Total Liabilities and Equity** | **4,194,726** | **3,969,288** | **3,875,126** | **3,451,745** |

The following sections are examples of descriptions and details that can be provided as information to fully inform a potential buyer of the facilities and capabilities of your company. Such sections would be included in a confidential review in order to fully inform the potential buyer of the features of the company. This comprehensive report about the company being offered is usually prepared for middle-market-sized businesses and is sometimes referred to as a confidential review, confidential business review, platform, or offering memorandum. They are sometimes leather- or spiral bound and sometimes distributed in CD-ROM or PDF format.

## Detailed Lists of Other Features

### Products

**The company produces products from over two thousand unique formulas. Current sales are approximately 65 percent cosmetic products, 20 percent specialty drinks, and 15 percent pharmaceuticals.**

**Products manufactured by the company include:**

- after-sun lotions and gels
- AHA creams and lotions
- analgesic rubs
- antiaging creams
- antidandruff products
- benzoyl peroxide creams and gels
- bleaching and fade-out creams
- capsicum pain relievers
- cellulite treatments

- collagen
- curl activator gels
- elastin, liposome, DHEA creams and lotions
- facial masks, scrubs, gels
- facial toners
- fragrances
- glycolic acid creams and lotions
- hair relaxers
- hair-setting lotions
- shampoos and conditioners
- shine gels
- styling gels
- suntan oils, creams, lotions
- tan accelerators

## Licenses

**The company is fully licensed by the following federal, state, and city regulatory agencies:**

- US Food and Drug Administration (FDA)
- State Department of Health Services
- Environmental Protection Agency (EPA)
- Bureau of Alcohol, Tobacco, and Firearms
- State Device Manufacturing (Medical Device)
- County Public Health Department

# Equipment and Furnishings

## Manufacturing Equipment

- (2) High-Speed Rotary Filling Machines for Liquids
- (2) High-Speed Tube Filling Machines—0.25 oz. to 12 oz.
- Duplex Pneumatic Piston Filler
- Admix Model DS-575 20 HP Shear Pump
- (10) Waukesha 1 ½" Stainless Steel Rotary Pumps
- 1 ½" Poly Pneumatic Diaphragm Pump
- (6) 1 ½" Sanitary Stainless Steel Centrifugal Pumps
- (3) Graco Monark Pneumatic Transfer Pumps
- Crepaco Model 3 HD 1 ½" Stainless Steel Rotary Pump
- Ertl Canister Filter w/ 1 HP Stainless Steel Gear Pump
- 1 ½" Peristaltic Hose Pump w/ DC Drive
- 12 qt. Planetary Mixer
- Webster's 750-gal. Triple-Agitated Stainless Steel Jacketed Mixer
- Century Machine Planetary Mixer
- Hobart Planetary Mixer
- Cowles Model W24 Dissolver 10 HP 200-gal. High Shear Mixer
- (4) Portable 250-gal. Stainless Steel Dome Top and Bottom Tanks
- (6) 60-gal. and 40-gal. Stainless Steel Kettles
- Legion Utensil 2000-gal. Stainless Steel Jacketed Dome Top
- CE Howard 1000-gal. S.S. Jacketed Dome Top and Bottom
- Feldmeier 1000-gal. S.S. Jacketed Dome Top and Bottom
- 20-gal. Stainless Steel Jacketed Kettle w/Pneumatic Agitator

- Crepace 1000-gal. S.S. Jacketed Dome Top and Bottom
- Feldmeier 900-gal. S.S. Jacketed Dome Top Double

**Packaging Equipment**

- Line #1: 12-Station Rotary Pressure Filler; Resins S20 Screw Capper; Pillar DB6114-4 Foiler; Videojet 37 Plus, Inkjet Coder w/Indexing Conveyor; Rotary Packout Disc and Interconnecting Conveyor
- Line #2: Biner Ellison 8-Station Rotary Pressure Filler; Kaps-All Screw Capper w/ Cap Feeder; Pillar2210R-BB6364-10 Foiler; Quadrel SL100 Sleever; Steam-Heated S.S. Heat Shrink Tunnel and Interconnecting Conveyor
- Line #3: Simplex 36" Rotary Disc Bottle Feeder; Simplex 900A1, 6-Head Inline-Pumped Pressure Filler; Pillar 221QR-BB6364-10 Foiler; Domino AtQD Inkjet Coder; Versapply Pressure-Sensitive Wraparound Labeler; OAL Heat Shrink Tunnel; Manual Packout Station; Best Pack MSD22-2 Top and Bottom Case Taper 001140 and Interconnecting Conveyor
- Line #4: 9-Head Inline-Pumped Pressure Filler; Simplex Mechanical Piston Filler; Kiss Packaging Systems VACT-06 Screw Capper; S.S. Packout Disc; Best Pack Top and Bottom Case Taper and Interconnecting Conveyor
- Line #5: 6-Head Inline Pumped Pressure Filler, Duplex Mechanical Piston Pump Filler, Videojet Excel Series 100, Inkjet Coder, CVC Model 40011 Pressure Sensitive Front and Back Labeler, Fleetline Top and Bottom Case Taper.

**Maintenance Equipment**

- Cincinnati 12 ½" X 42" Engine Lathe
- H-frame press
- table saw
- drill press

**Warehouse and Shipping Equipment**

- Wultec Model WHP-150 Semi-Automatic Pallet Stretch Wrapper
- O'Haus Digital Platform Scale
- HOMS Mechanical Platform Scale
- (2) Avery Digital Platform Scales
- (2) Cat Model GC25, 5000-lb. L.P.G. Forklifts

**Laboratory Equipment**

- Shimadzu Model LC-20AD HPLC
- Shimadzu Model TDC-VE Total Organic Carbon Analyzer
- Shimadzu GC-8A Gas Chromatograph
- Shimadzu UV-240 Visible Recording Spectrophotometer
- Shimadzu UV-1700 UV-VIS Spectrophotometer
- Shimadzu IR-435 Infrared Spectrophotometer
- Metrohm Model 836 Titrando Titrator
- Avantar 360 Infrared Spectrophotometer
- Avatar 36AFT-IR Thermo Nicolet
- Cambridge Photozoom Inverted Microscope

### Owners and Management Staff

| Title | Name | Owner percent | Since | Salary |
|---|---|---|---|---|
| CEO and President | | 76 percent | 1970 | $150,000 |
| Vice President and G.M. | | 10 percent | 1989 | $70,000 |
| Chief Operating Officer | | 5 percent | 2008 | $80,000 |
| Investor | | 5 percent | | |
| Controller | | | 2001 | $55,000 |
| Production Manager | | | 2008 | $70,000 |
| Director of Purchasing | | 4 percent | 1991 | $60,000 |

## Other Information to Be Disclosed

A next step in the process may include a walkthrough of the company facilities and face-to-face meeting with company owners. Throughout the process, the owner must determine what level of information about the company should be divulged without a letter of intent or purchase offer at a specific price and terms. If there is no hope in sight of reaching an agreement of the value of the company, there is no point in providing proprietary information about the company. Information that is not divulged in the early stages of the process can be considered contingencies of the transaction and can be provided to the satisfaction of the buyer prior to a final agreement being executed. These contingencies provide the buyer the right to terminate the agreement for lack of satisfaction with the information not previously disclosed. These important issues will vary with different types of businesses and the critical nature of the information requested. In many cases, the information is essential for a potential buyer in order to justify the time and expense of fully evaluating the company for the intended purpose.

In general, the offering of a business for sale process with a professional who specializes in such transactions involves a listing agreement for a period of six months to two years, payment of up-front fees for valuation, preparation, advertising and marketing, and comprehensive information about the company including the history, the owners, the products or services provided, the opportunity features sought by typical buyers, the financial history, current financial results, future plans for growth, and an overview of the industry and industry trends. The unique features of a company and the future prospects for the industry are important considerations and should be detailed favorably to define the company's future potential value.

## Case History: Beware of Misleading Intentions and Financing Mistakes

> A company in the marble and granite fabrication industry engaged me to offer the company for sale. The company had a long history and had been growing steadily for many years. The company was prepared for an offering, it was marketed heavily, and it attracted several potential acquirers. One of the interested parties seemed willing to pay the asking price, providing the owner would cooperate with his immigration visa application, which required him to make an investment of a specified size in the country that employed workers. The buyer was familiar with the construction industry, and it was felt that he was qualified to run the company.

> A purchase and sale agreement was executed, and the funding process began. The buyer had an adequate down payment but had difficulty in obtaining the financing locally due to a lack of citizenship in the country. The buyer asked the seller to finance the remainder of the purchase price. The discussions regarding a seller note finally led to an earn-out arrangement, whereby the buyer agreed to pay seller 10 percent of all sales for a period of years. The seller agreed to this arrangement in spite of my informing him that many accountants consider a 10 percent fee off the top as excessive and not financially feasible in a competitive industry where profit margins are limited.
>
> But the deal closed, and the buyer took possession. The seller continued to work with the buyer, who was in his former country most of the time or engaging in building projects locally, and his family members, who were more often present than the buyer. His family members had no business management experience. The downward spiral had already begun. Within six months, they were no longer paying the seller his commission on sales, forcing him to commence legal action. He finally got the company back through foreclosure. The equipment had not been properly maintained, the customer base had disintegrated, and few employees were left with the experience to do the work.

So a good company sold to someone who seemed to be the right kind of person ended up back in the seller's hands—with a seriously reduced value. The buyer either just wanted an entry into the country, which would be misleading intentions, or made poor management decisions. The generous earn-out arrangement attracted the seller, and he ignored the potential damage due to failure, a mistake in financing the sale of the company.

# CHAPTER 12

## *Implementing the Marketing Plan*

Once the company is prepared for sale, the marketing method has been determined, a marketing plan is completed, and information has been prepared for dissemination to interested parties, it is time to implement the marketing plan.

As interested parties are attracted through the marketing plan, they should be responded to promptly and professionally. One thing to remember is that time kills all deals.

### Dissemination of Information

For most business owners, confidentiality is very important. For initial inquiries, it is best to respond with a blind flyer, which can be sent via e-mail. This will give most inquirers enough basic information to decide if the offering fits their priorities and criteria. If it does, it will probably be followed with an e-mail or phone call with questions or a request to tour the facilities. And in this event, it is generally recommended to request information on the inquirer regarding background, financial capability, and level of interest. If the inquirer doesn't seem to fit the basic qualifications necessary to acquire the company or to operate it, there is no need to disclose additional information about the company, expose confidentiality, and disturb the feeling of job security and dedication to duty of your employees.

Requiring information from the potential buyer can have another benefit to your advantage. It discourages some of those who are willing to waste your time when they really aren't likely to acquire the company. There are those who are just looking for something too good to be true or looking for information about your operations so they can compete with you. Those aren't the interested parties with whom you want to spend your time and to whom you want to expose your business and reveal your trade secrets and your mode of operation.

As far as financial information is concerned, you may want to provide a summary profit and loss statement or simply mention the level of revenue on the blind flyer. Any additional financial information can then be disclosed after your buyer qualification and level of interest has been determined.

## Meeting with Potential Buyers

The inquirer, if interest continues, will want to visit the facilities and have a meeting with the owner. Again, this should normally not be done until you are convinced of the buyer's level of interest and qualifications for acquisition and ownership. Once those have been established, a meeting could be arranged at such time as you feel comfortable with the exposure and protection of confidentiality with your employees. If such is not a problem, you can meet most anytime. If it is of concern, you could arrange a meeting and tour at such time as the employees are not present.

It is important when agreeing to meet with potential buyers to limit uninvited visitors. There are many occasions when a purported buyer will visit a seller's facilities and bring along anyone he or she wants. This has sometimes turned out to be an unrecognized competitor who wants to see your operation. At that point, confidentiality is immediately exposed and can be broadcast throughout your industry and area of operation, as well as to your employees. You should practice damage control at all times when arranging visits to your facilities.

## Financial Reviews

It is generally not recommended to allow any audit of your records until the negotiation is completed and the offer of purchase has been submitted and accepted. This is done in due diligence and can be a contingency of the deal. In this case, the buyer would have an out if there were disapproval of the results of the audit or inspection of records.

Audits and inspection of records can be an unavoidable cause of exposure of confidentiality with your employees, another valid reason for avoidance until the transaction is accepted and ready to close.

## Observing Operations

It is also not a good idea to allow an interested party to be present at the business to observe operations or verify sales results until such time as an offer has been accepted and due diligence has been nearly completed. No matter what reason is given to employees for some stranger to be observing the operation, it doesn't take long for them to figure it out. Once it is figured out, the reason they were given is exposed as misleading and certainly does not enhance employee relations. This can cause bad feelings going forward with the sale or in continuing operations if the deal fails.

## Interviewing Employees

It is of utmost importance throughout the marketing process to avoid disturbing the operation of the business and creating a feeling of abandonment by the employees. Sometimes it is better to divulge your plans to key employees; sometimes it isn't. This depends entirely upon each individual situation. If it isn't divulged, care should be taken not to do collateral damage in the process.

One important caution is to avoid potential buyers interviewing your employees or even conversing with them. A breakdown in deal negotiation could result in a raid on your gifted employees, damaging you in a failed process.

# CHAPTER 13

## *Negotiating the Terms and Conditions*

At such time as an interested party is ready to move to the next level and acquire your company, the terms of sale must be negotiated. This process usually begins with a letter of intent or purchase agreement submitted by the buyer.

### Terms and Conditions to Be Negotiated

Once a letter of intent or purchase agreement is signed by the buyer and submitted to the seller, the terms can be negotiated. These include but are not limited to:

- **Purchase price:** This is the total price to be paid for the company in cash, financing, or other means.
- **Deposit:** This is a deposit into escrow, which is refundable if escrow is terminated or becomes a part of the cash down payment if escrow closes. This is sometimes called an earnest deposit, simply displaying sincerity of the intent of consummating the acquisition. Additional deposits are sometimes required at various stages of the escrow process. Deposits can be refundable or nonrefundable if the contract fails. They are usually refundable during early stages and

can sometimes become nonrefundable at some point in the escrow process.

- **Down payment:** This is the cash down payment, a part of the purchase price, to be paid into escrow by the buyer prior to closing, usually upon acceptance of all terms and conditions.
- **Financing:** This would define the amount and type of financing to be obtained by the buyer, such as a commercial bank loan, SBA loan, seller financing, or earn-out payments to the seller. Financing terms normally include a date for required credit approval, which would be a letter of commitment from the lender. The seller could extend the date for approval if it is not provided by the stated date, or the seller could terminate the transaction.
- **Type of sale:** This could be a sale of stock or an asset sale. The structure of the sale could be very important for the buyer and seller for taxation purposes. A *stock sale* would leave the corporation intact and result in possible capital gain or loss for the seller based upon the sale price and the seller's basis in the stock. An *asset sale* could result in a capital gain or loss for the individual seller if the company is a sole proprietorship, the partners if it is a partnership, or the corporation if a corporate sale of assets. An asset sale could provide the opportunity for the buyer to depreciate the assets for tax purposes. A stock sale probably would not except for remaining depreciation of assets or any newly acquired assets in the corporation. All of the taxation considerations should be discussed with accountants for the parties for this mutually important agreement.
- **Due diligence:** This is a period of time, usually defined in the agreement, during which the buyer can review

financial statements, sales records, staffing, leases, and other documents; inspect the facilities for operable conditions; verify inventory; and examine other features of the company. There are often contingencies for these reviews and inspections with the buyer's right to approve or disapprove, terms for the seller to correct deficiencies to the buyer's satisfaction, and termination provisions for the buyer in the case of any uncorrected disapprovals.

- **Assets included in sale:** It is important to identify the assets included, such as cash, accounts receivable, inventory, furniture, fixtures, equipment, facilities, goodwill, intangible assets, leasehold improvements, computer programs, business records, customer lists, intellectual property, and other assets.
- **Assets not included in sale:** It is important to identify assets not included, such as cash, accounts receivable, inventory, furniture, fixtures, equipment, facilities, goodwill, intangible assets, leasehold improvements, computer programs, business records, customer lists, intellectual property, and other assets.
- **Liabilities to be assumed by buyer:** Liabilities that the buyer is assuming should be identified, such as bank loans, accounts payable, personal loans, equipment leases, facility leases, product liability, and other liabilities.
- **Taxation considerations:** Taxation of the proceeds for the seller and future taxation for the buyer can be important parts of the structure of sale, and both parties should fully understand it. A review by each party's accountant is usually advisable.
- **Lease assignment terms:** All leases or other legal obligations that the buyer is assuming from the seller should be identified in the agreement. These should include facility, equipment,

or vehicle leases; vendor agreements; employee commitments; and other legal commitments.

- **Representations and warranties:** Representations and warranties involve disclosure of information of the parties to each other, such as assets, indebtedness, litigation, contracts, environmental matters, and employee commitments, that is, virtually any matter that one party could divulge to the other that could have an effect on the transaction. With transactions on larger companies and some middle-market companies, this section will provide for cancellation provisions and indemnification from the breaching party.
- **Noncompete agreement:** This is the seller's agreement not to compete with the buyer in the same business or area for a specified period of time.
- **Date of closing and possession:** This is the specific date of closing with allowance for unintentional delays.

## Importance of Counsel

Before final agreement to terms and conditions, each party should engage counsel of an attorney and accountant, if necessary, in order to fully understand the ramifications of the terms and conditions. This can prevent costly mistakes and reduce the danger of last-minute hitches that can delay or prevent closing of the sale.

## Seller Financing

The seller should give serious thought before agreeing to carry a large part of the purchase price as a seller note. The danger is in having to repossess the business for nonpayment. If this occurs, the seller may not be in a position to resume operation of the business. The seller may receive the business in a damaged condition. The employees may have gone. The customers may have gone. The equipment may be damaged. The reputation may be destroyed.

On the other hand, lenders often feel uncomfortable making a loan if the seller is not carrying part of the loan. They sometimes feel a lack of confidence on the part of the seller that the buyer can make a go of it. This must be a consideration for the seller because it could make a sale not feasible without some seller financing.

One important aspect of this consideration is that, if the seller provides a seller note and the buyer is obtaining other financing, the seller note will always be subordinated to the other loan. This means that, if the buyer quits paying, your only recourse as the seller is to pay off the first lender and foreclose on your note, all of which can be risky, stressful, undesirable, and perhaps impossible.

## Case History: Failure of Negotiation

The following case emphasizes the possible effect of obstinate posturing. It also provides a textbook case of too many eggs in one basket.

> I was counseling with a manufacturer of metal fabrications in a Western state that was seeking a sale or merger as a source of survival due to undercapitalization and loss of their biggest customer. The company was distressed after a forty-year history manufacturing aftermarket van body equipment for service vehicles. Sales had declined in recent years due to a scaling back of new vehicle purchases by the customer who represented a large portion of the

business of the company. The slowdown in business made a valuation of the company unattractive for a buyer interested in a going operation with a reliable stream of income.

Due to this factor alone, the seller's best source of a buyer was to attract another company in the industry interested in expanding into the area or growing his or her business through acquisition of companies with a different customer base or product line. Although the initial cost of such expansion can be expensive, the benefits are generally reliable, immediate, and lasting.

Two promising buyers expressed an interest in the company, one on the West Coast and the other on the East Coast. Both parties were interested in a merger or acquisition, and both desired for the principal of the company to stay on to run the operation for a period of time.

The company owner also owned the two industrial buildings the company occupied and serviced the mortgages of the properties with rent paid to himself by the company. The mortgages were in default due to the financial difficulty the company was experiencing. There was a possibility of one or both of the interested parties retaining the leases on the buildings. The mortgage company was threatening foreclosure.

The company had some automated, state-of-the-art production equipment that provided excellent quality. The equipment loan was in default, and the lender was threatening foreclosure. One of the interested parties submitted an offer that would have provided the owner with a continuing source of income by working with the buyer's company, the probability of an assumption of the loans on the equipment, and a purchase of much of the other equipment and furnishings of the company. There was also a specified payment amount for goodwill. The owner, against my advice, elected not to respond to the offer. He was too proud of his company although it was in much distress.

The other interested party was requesting additional information. This party was financially capable of making the acquisition and needed such a facility on the West Coast; however, the seller had some previous experience with him and was reluctant to proceed unless all other possibilities were exhausted.

The owner felt that, in lieu of a buyer for his company, he could sell the equipment and real estate and discontinue the operation, leaving him comfortable in retirement. He ignored my advice to pursue the two interested parties due to the fact that, if his company and his real estate ended up in foreclosure, he would lose control of any ultimate sale of either and could be disappointed with the outcome. He was represented by an attorney who was giving him legal advice as well.

> The lenders filed for repossession of the equipment and real estate and published notices of sales of the collateral. The owner then had to file personal bankruptcy in an attempt to delay the sales. The bankruptcy forced an auction of all of the equipment and furnishings. The court forced a listing of the buildings for sale.

So this story is about negotiating, which is what this owner chose not to do.

Obstinacy is not a good posture when you are not negotiating from a position of strength. Negotiation is not always successful, but refusal to negotiate is usually not the best course. Good negotiation would probably have turned this situation into a win-win for all parties. Obstinate posturing prevented it.

The other textbook case this story emphasizes is the case of lack of diversity of customer base, that is, too much concentration of customer base. Over many years, this company perfected the design of their product line of van conversions for the cable TV industry. The customer base was spread among numerous customers in the industry for many years, but through consolidation and monopolization in the industry, their customer base continually became more concentrated until 80 percent of their business was to one customer in that industry. Yes, 80 percent. That meant that, if that customer left, they would lose 80 percent of their business overnight.

This, of course, would be fatal for any manufacturer, no matter what industry they were serving. When this behemoth company decided to buy this product from one source exclusively in another part of the country, a region that better served their national fleet of vehicles, the company lost 80 percent of their business, a perfect example of too many eggs in one basket.

# CHAPTER 14

## *Due Diligence and Documentation Provided at Sale*

### Due Diligence

An important and sometimes time-consuming part of the negotiation and acceptance process is what is called due diligence, a period of time and an opportunity for the buyer to diligently examine the company to verify the features of the company and confirm the decision to consummate the acquisition. Due diligence actually begins in the early stages of dissemination of information to potential buyers but is of utmost of importance upon an acceptance of a sale agreement.

### Financial Due Diligence

Financial due diligence involves examining financial statements, such as balance sheets, income statements, cash flow statements, tax returns, bank records, sales reports, customer invoices, expense invoices, and other records to verify past performance. This is a brief process for small businesses but can be an onerous task for larger businesses.

Much of this process may have been completed during the investigation of the company prior to the purchase agreement. After the terms and conditions are agreed upon is the time that due diligence becomes of utmost importance for the buyer. The better you, the seller, have the financial information ready for a sale, the smoother the financial due diligence will go. The buyer will want to be assured of the true financial condition of the company. This is generally the case regardless of which assets and liabilities are included in the sale. Buyer's investigation of the financial condition can be invaluable to the buyer for assurance that the company's financial health reflects the historic success that has been reviewed in the decision to buy the company. A more thorough investigation of liabilities can reveal decisions made for tax or sale purposes that are misleading and overstate the past performance of the company. This is not only important for the buyer but for the seller as well. If the company fails to perform well after closing, the buyer may become aware of undisclosed information that, should there have been a disclosure, would have resulted in a different decision regarding the acquisition or a different valuation of the company.

If the buyer's investigation of the financials reveals alarming information, it may require an audit of the financial condition of the company. Expensive and time consuming, this can delay the process to the point of "time kills all deals." So it is important to have the books in order and all matters of importance to the buyer disclosed up front and easily verified.

When the buyer's accountant reviews the seller's income statement and balance sheet, he or she will be looking for verification of the net income, the cash flow, and the trends and irregularities that may be apparent. The accountant will want to compare current assets and liabilities with historic figures to verify adequate working capital and current liquidity ratio, the financial ratio that may indicate the ability of the company to meet its financial obligations in a timely manner. If there is bank or SBA financing involved, the current and quick ratio can make or break financing of the transaction.

## Case History: Watch Out for Red Flags

The following is a simple example of the type of red flags that can become important in due diligence.

> The owner of a company selling and installing car stereos, custom wheels, and other auto accessories engaged me. I reviewed the financial statements that he provided.

| | 2010 | 2011 |
|---|---|---|
| Sales | $1,320,489 | $1,315,002 |
| Cost of goods sold | | |
| Beginning inventory | 215,000 | 772,007 |
| Purchases | 604,588 | 573,396 |
| Ending inventory | (386,538) | (714,262) |
| Total cost of goods | 443,050 | 631,141 |
| Gross profit | 877,439 | 683,861 |
| Operating expenses | 575,753 | 381,640 |
| Net Income | 301,686 | 302,221 |

> Sales were level over a two-year period at $1.3 million. Costs of goods sold were $443,000 and $631,000, respectively. Gross profits were $877,000 and $683,000, respectively. Operating expenses were level at $300,000. Net income was level at $302,000. From a quick glance,

this may look all well and good. The financial statement reflected gross profit margins of 67 percent and 53 percent, very healthy profit margins. Maybe it was too good to be true. It reflected net income margins of 23 percent, very healthy bottom lines. Most companies would only strive for such levels of financial performance.

However, looking in more detail, the beginning inventory in the first year was $215,000, and the ending inventory was $386,000. No problem there. But the beginning inventory in the second year was $772,000, which was impossible. You can't have an increase in inventory from one day to the next of 100 percent without it being reflected in purchases or adjustments. This discrepancy is an obvious red flag. If such a situation had occurred, it would have necessitated adjustments that are not reflected in the statements provided. Another abnormality that would require some scrutiny and explanation is that the net income was level but the gross profit margins were off by $180,000. Not a normal situation.

The store was open seven days per week from 9:00 a.m. until 9:00 p.m. That is 360 hours per month. The staffing levels at the store would add up to 1,800 or more hours per month. The payroll plus payroll taxes and workers comp insurance would be $225,000 to $300,000.

The income statement reflected salaries and wages of $250,000 the first year and $100,000 the second year. Of this amount, $40,000 each year was allocated to owner's salary. The owner declared that he didn't work there. The obvious inaccuracy in reporting the wages and salaries is another red flag.

It is possible that all of these concerns could be explained to the satisfaction of a buyer; however, an audit of the financials and a complete inventory would be in order, as well as a review of payroll and sales tax reports to the state. The numbers need to add up, especially with inexplicable red flags.

Whether you are selling or buying a business, you should be aware of the importance of the buyer's need to have a reliable understanding of the company, whether investigated entirely by the buyer or experienced professionals who know what red flags to be aware of and to watch for in the financial review.

## Legal and Contractual Due Diligence

Legal due diligence can involve review of information regarding any past or pending legal issues involving the company, including lawsuits or claims, facility and equipment leases, lending instruments, employment contracts, customer sales agreements, and other agreements that could affect the future operation of the company. It can include the right of the seller to sell or assign the assets or shares of stock.

The buyer will want to investigate lease commitments and future lease options, which can have an adverse effect on future income. The buyer will want to search for legal claims and liabilities to determine any pending or potential claims or legal actions. The buyer will want to investigate any possibility of product warranty claims or obligations and verify insurance protection for future claims.

The buyer will want to investigate any possibility of employment claims, any contractual employee obligations, any union contracts, and pending or potential claims of discrimination or injury. The buyer will want to investigate workers comp insurance policies to verify potential responsibility for prior claims or unreported injuries.

## Operational Due Diligence

Operational due diligence involves an observance of operations, including processes, sales, services, and administrative functions of the company. It can include a review of employees, employment policies, benefits, and employment contracts.

The buyer may want to investigate the company's utilization of the latest technologies in order to maintain competitiveness, as well as the conditions of facilities and furniture, fixtures, and equipment for adequacy for continuing operations. The buyer may want to investigate any potential hazardous waste possibilities or violation of any regulations regarding hazardous material usage or other environmental considerations.

Due diligence for small companies is normally done between the buyer and the seller in the seller's facilities or between the accountants of the parties. Due diligence for larger companies becomes more complex and comprehensive and requires much more time and many more participants, sometimes transpiring for months. Regardless of the difficulty of the process, the ultimate importance of verification and disclosure makes it all worthwhile and imperative for any sale of a company.

Due diligence must occur while there is a contingency in the purchase and sale agreement that provides for an option of cancellation of the agreement if there are discoveries that do not meet the satisfaction of the buyer that the seller is either unable or unwilling to correct to the buyer's satisfaction.

## Documentation Provided at Sale

- **Purchase and sale agreement:** Documentation of the sale usually occurs in escrow or with the assistance of a closing attorney once the purchase and sale agreement is negotiated and executed. Once this document is executed, the agreement should define all of the terms and conditions, and the closing attorney or escrow agent works from the executed document.
- **Searches and clearances:** During the closing process of a business transfer, the escrow agent or attorney should conduct searches and clearances for creditor claims, tax clearances for assurance of timely payment of all taxes due, verification of the legal capacity of the seller to convey title, any pending litigation of the company, any undisclosed assignments of assets, or other legal issues. These searches and clearances are imperative to assure clear title to the assets being transferred.
- **Bill of sale:** A bill of sale is included in an asset sale, which should list all of the assets being sold. This document will be included in the UCC filing with the secretary of state if a security agreement and promissory note are recorded. This is important for the protection of any lender involved or any possible future buyer of the assets.
- **Promissory note:** A promissory note must be included for any portion of the purchase price being provided as seller financing. If there is third-party lending, the promissory note will be provided by the lender and executed between the lender and the buyer.

- **Security agreement:** A security agreement is usually required for UCC filings with the state for the protection of the lender and anyone who intends to acquire or take assignment of the assets.
- **Allocation of assets:** In an asset sale, an allocation of assets must be included in order to provide an accurate basis for taxation for both parties. This is important in terms of recapture of depreciation and capital gain for the seller and depreciation for the buyer. The Internal Revenue Service requires this document.
- **Inventory list:** An inventory list should be provided between the buyer and seller in order to adjust inventory for the seller and establish inventory for the buyer, both for accounting purposes. This is necessary in order to provide accurate bases for financial statements for the parties.
- **Representations and warranties:** A representation and warranties agreement is often used in larger company sales to cover representations that the seller has made in terms of legal claims and issues, product liability and licensing issues, condition of assets, relationships with employees and customers, and other matters. It would normally cover any and all matters of disclosure between the parties. There is sometimes a provision for penalties for breaches of such warranties and representations.
- **Noncompetition agreement:** A noncompetition agreement is usually a part of a business transfer. The buyer usually wants assurance that the seller will not compete in the same business or area or with the same customers for a specified period of time. The length of the period of time of such agreements is sometimes regulated in the given state.

- **Employment agreement:** An employment agreement may be required if the seller agrees to stay on to assist the buyer during a period of transition or for a longer period. There could also be an agreement with certain employees that the buyer feels that the success of the business is contingent upon.
- **Lease assignment:** A lease assignment is imperative if the buyer intends to continue to operate from the same premises. In some cases, a specified long-term occupancy is critical to support the value of the company, particularly in the case of a retail or restaurant establishment.

The following case history regarding lease assignment provides an example of the importance of the assurance of lease assignment.

## Case History of Failure to Deliver

> The owner of a private school engaged me to sell the company. The school had been established for fifteen years and had a good reputation in the area. They occupied a five-thousand-square-foot freestanding building, which they had fully equipped for the school, under a short-term lease. The company reported annual revenue of $500,000 and annual earnings of $120,000. They taught kindergarten through second grade. Because of the reputation of the school and the positive growth of the private school industry, the company was offered at $450,000.
>
> The marketing information was compiled, marketing materials were prepared, and the marketing plan ensued. After several months of communication with interested

> parties, facility tours, and negotiations, an agreement of sale was executed. The seller had assured me and all interested parties that he had an excellent relationship with the landlord and the landlord had agreed to extend the lease, assigning it to the buyer. This was a contingency of the sale, as relocating the school would have a serious impact on the sustainability of the income, and the cost of relocating would be prohibitive for the buyer.
>
> As it turned out, the seller was unable to get the lease assignment because they had been delinquent in rent on numerous occasions and did not have a good relationship with the landlord. This situation could not be rectified, and the sale of the business failed. The seller had assured the buyer and me that he had obtained the right to assign the lease from the landlord. The seller had not been truthful and could not deliver. Not only was the seller unable to sell the school, he was determined to be the cause of the termination of the sale and was compelled to pay the contracted fee as if the sale had been completed.

It can be costly to make promises you cannot keep in order to get agreement to sell on the assumption that you can get the needed cooperation from third parties. This business had little value if it had to be relocated. There was no availability of other facilities in the immediate area. Moving to another area would have cost a considerable sum for facility improvements and would have required an entirely new student base due to moving out of the area.

This was a case of misrepresentation and failure to deliver.

## Professional Counselors

Depending upon the size and type of business being transferred, various professionals may be required to assure appropriate examination and planning of the structure of the sale. These may include a CPA or an attorney for tax matters, an attorney for estate planning, an attorney for review of intellectual property protection, environmental specialists for possible risks, and an attorney for review of closing documents.

---

### EXAMPLE OF PURCHASE AND SALE AGREEMENT

**Some terms of a Purchase and Sale Agreement would be as follows:**

This Agreement dated ____________________, ______ is by and between ______________________________________ ("Buyer") and ______________________________________, ("Seller") for the purchase and sale of assets of:
Business Name ______________________________________
Located at __________________________________________
City ________________ St______ Zip _________ ("Business")
Purchase Price __________________________________Dollars
$ ______________ payable as follows:
Initial Deposit upon acceptance by Seller ________________
$___________ to be deposited with escrow company.
Deposit upon opening of escrow $ ____________________ to be deposited with escrow company.

Balance of Down Payment $ ____________________ collected funds to be deposited with escrow before closing.
Seller Financing on business assets $____________________
monthly payments of $ __________ for ____ months @ ____ percent.
Other Financing by bank or SBA $____________________
Financing not to be a contingency of sale unless agreed by seller.
Assumption of notes or payables $____________________
Total Purchase Price $____________________

Assets included in the sale of the business shall include, but are not limited to, equipment, trade fixtures, leaseholds, leasehold improvements, contract rights, business records, licenses, franchises, goodwill, covenant not to compete, trade secrets, trade names, fictitious business names, logos, distributorship rights, transferable licenses and permits, copyrights, patents, telephone numbers, supplies, works in progress, and inventory. Inventory is estimated at a cost of $______________ and shall be valued at closing by agreement between Buyer and Seller. Any increase or decrease shall then be adjusted first against seller financing and then against down payment. Other assets included:

______________________________________________________

Assets not included shall be accounts receivable, bank accounts, deposits, cash, and financial records. Other assets not included:

______________________________________________________

It is recommended that a purchase agreement form be used that has been prepared by a professional organization familiar with the legal issues in business transfers. Such organizations could be the International Business Brokers Association or your local association of realtors. If you employ an attorney, the form may not be necessary, as he or she may prefer to prepare the documents personally.

Many other forms utilized in the sale of businesses are available from online or local sources. If you prepare such forms without professional assistance, it is recommended that you have an attorney familiar with business transfers such as bulk sales or stock sales review them. The laws in your state may require some professional assistance, especially in the case of a sale of stock.

A sale of stock is sometimes required to be transferred by an attorney or an investment banker who is licensed as a securities dealer and operates under the regulations of the Security and Exchange Commission.

# CHAPTER 15

## *Integrating the Buyer*

### Importance

Integration is much more important than may be fully realized by many parties to a sale of a business. This realization becomes more important once ownership and operations change hands and is sometimes overlooked in the negotiating process.

### Goodwill

One of the profound statements quoted in the business sales industry is, "If the goodwill walks out the door with the seller, you have nothing to sell." This is self-explanatory. Most businesses, especially small ones, are built on personal relationships between the principal party who founded and operates the business and the primary customers. In order for the buyer to be successful after taking over the operation of the company, the primary customers must be retained, and those relationships must be conveyed by the seller and carried forward by the new owner.

## Vendors

This same situation holds true for vendors of the company. Although this may be less urgent than the customer base, vendors or suppliers can be most important in retaining quality and performance. The loss of a key vendor for an important material, part, product, or service can be crucial in some businesses. If such is the case, assurance should be made of a continuation of the vendor source for the buyer. Otherwise, the loss of the source could reduce the value of the company.

## Employees

The other critical element of integration is the relationship with the employees. Sellers usually maintain a personal relationship with their employees. They know all of them and are familiar with their personalities, their likes and dislikes, and their relationships with the other employees and their relationships with customers. It is critical for employee integration to work smoothly if the company is to continue to operate successfully. The seller can be instrumental in making this transition go smoothly.

## Training and Transition Assistance

It is often important for the seller to stay on in a training capacity for a period of time in order to assure a smooth transition of operational, personality, and relationship integration. Sometimes, the seller will stay on for an indefinite period to assure retention of the customer base, smooth continuation of operations, and training of new management and to provide a stable and sustainable company going forward.

## Case History: Importance of Customer Retention

This case emphasizes the disaster of lack of customer retention.

> I was working with a local plumbing company as a business advisor in evaluating and positioning the company for a sale. Prior to a complete evaluation of the company, one of the two partners informed me of a possible sale of the company to another local plumbing company. The selling company was established in a plumbing specialty of jetting of waste lines, which required special high-pressure equipment and techniques, and they were well equipped. They had numerous contracts for preventative maintenance, which provided steady income for the company.
>
> The buying company owner had been in the plumbing business for some time but only a short while as an owner. The owners worked together somewhat. The selling company owners had some health problems and desired to retire. The buying company was seeking a reliable source of business with a good profit margin.
>
> The two company ownerships had arrived at an agreement to sell the jetting company for $1.2 million. The financial reports that I had reviewed previously did not reflect income adequate to support such a sale price, but when

discussing it with the sellers, I was assured that the buyer was fully aware of everything about the company and was anxious to merge the two operations immediately.

The contracts were prepared, along with disclosures and a waiver of valuations and appraisals. The seller was receiving a $300,000 down payment and was carrying a seller note for $900,000 with monthly payments for a number of years to come.

A few days before closing was scheduled, the seller informed me that their largest customer, who represented 25 percent of their revenue, had canceled their contract due to budgetary constraints. I informed seller that we must meet and disclose this to the buyer. It was decided that the sale price would be reduced by 25 percent and the seller note adjusted accordingly.

So the escrow closed, and the buyer took possession of the company. The seller partner, the primary customer retention part of the company, had a stroke and was unable to assist with integration, which, in this case, was critical in retaining the customer base. The other partner tried to help but also had health problems and was unable to be of much help.

The buyer lost additional customers to aggressive competitors and very soon was unable to meet the payment obligations with seller. No agreement was reached

> to resolve the issue, so the buyer walked away and left the business inoperable.
>
> We arranged another meeting. The sellers agreed to again reduce the note payable, significantly in fact, in order for the buyer to continue operating. The two reductions in the purchase price brought the price more in line with a prudent purchase price for the assets acquired, based on the income previously reported by the seller.

So the lessons from this case come down to making sure the sale price is supported by the income, the payment terms can be met in the event of a downturn, and integration is an essential part of the process. If integration had been addressed more aggressively in this case, it could have turned out a lot better for the buyer and the seller. Lack of customer retention can be tragic.

# CONCLUSION

In conclusion, we should review the major points to commit to memory regarding the process of selling a business. The intent of this book is to give a potential seller of a company a basic knowledge of the elements and considerations that are important in the sale of a business and an outline and source of reference of the process.

## The Essentials in Review

- **The objectives of the seller:** The objectives you wish to accomplish by selling your company should be determined before the other steps in the sale process are initiated. Otherwise, the entire process may be a waste of time and effort and mislead potential buyers into a time-consuming process that is destined to fail. If the equation doesn't compute satisfactorily, you can either rethink your objectives or continue running your company until the equation works.
- **The value of the company:** The valuation of the company is the key to a successful transaction. It should compensate the seller adequately for the company based upon the value of the earnings or assets. It should provide an acquisition that will compensate the buyer adequately for the time, effort, and financial commitment. It should establish the price that a ready, willing, and able buyer and seller can agree to be the fair market value of the enterprise.

- **The preparation for sale:** In order to show the company in its best light, it should be prepared properly. It should be showtime, legally, operationally, and financially prepared.
- **The offering of the sale of the company:** You should decide the best way to offer the company for sale and how it will be presented, packaged, and marketed, whether the company or a professional in the business of selling businesses performs it. In most all cases, I would recommend a carefully selected professional with a good reputation of performance and integrity.
- **The marketing plan:** Either you or a professional representative should prepare a comprehensive marketing plan in order to attract the best potential buyers for the company.
- **The information provided about the company:** Comprehensive information must be prepared and provided for the buyer to fully evaluate the acquisition. You must be able to assure the buyer that the company is sound and will provide the buyer's objectives.
- **The implementation of the marketing plan:** The marketing plan must be implemented to attract the attention desired from your targeted audience of potential buyers. Caution should be exercised in protecting confidentiality.
- **The negotiation of the terms and conditions:** Negotiation of all terms and conditions is essential in completing the transaction while guarding against seller's remorse or buyer's anxiety, either of which can kill a worthwhile transition.
- **The due diligence and documentation of the sale:** A legal counsel or an experienced business escrow agent should complete or review all documentation. The documentation

should protect both parties and respect all legal issues that can affect the parties, including matters of taxation.

- **The integration of the buyer with customers, employees, and vendors:** Integration of the buyer with your employees, vendors, and customers becomes the key element of the process once the documents are executed, the money changes hands, and the buyer takes over control of the company. This becomes the final concern of a successful transfer of a company.

## Lessons and Key Words

A sale of a company can be quite simple or very complex. It can be quick or as slow as molasses on a cold day. It can be successful or a nightmare for both parties. The important thing is to avoid collateral damage in a failed process.

To make your transfer of ownership successful, take it a step at a time, and don't skip any steps. And remember some of the key words that were highlighted and the associated lessons:

- **Usually it doesn't sell:** Many practitioners in the business sale industry testify that only about 20 percent of businesses listed for sale actually sell. This statistic should emphasize the need to follow all of the essential steps, from an accurate valuation to preparation to marketing to implementation to integration.
- **Ready, willing, and able:** Successful transfers of companies occur with a ready, willing, and able buyer and seller. Value, purchase price, and terms and conditions are determined likewise.

- **First things first:** Make sure the seller's objectives can be met by selling the company.
- **You only get one chance to make a first impression:** Initial contact is all important whether you are selling your company or opening your restaurant.
- **Get it ready to sell:** Get your company showtime, operationally, and financially ready to sell.
- **A good place to work:** Make your company look and feel like a good place to work, including physically and operationally.
- **Control the collateral damage:** Be cautious about collateral damage in terms of confidentiality. Competitors can undermine you if they lack scruples.
- **Do not misrepresent:** Misrepresentation only leads to pain in the future. Liability for misrepresentation can cost more than your company value. Misrepresentation doesn't require dishonesty or lack of scruples. It can happen accidently or unintentionally. Make sure what you represent or present is factual and verifiable and discloses potential successes or pitfalls.
- **Time kills all deals:** Be timely in responding to inquiries and providing requested information about the company. Without it, the interest will grow cold, and the deal won't happen.
- **Size matters:** The value of a company grows exponentially with size. Small companies are priced accordingly due to their fragile nature and their less certain future.
- **Sanity test:** The sanity test is a good way to determine if the asking price is achievable and makes sense for a buyer. This test can provide support for the valuation of your company.

- **If the goodwill walks out with the seller, there is nothing to sell:** The success of your business may depend upon your personal relationships with your customers. If that is the case, that is your goodwill, and the goodwill must be conveyed over to the buyer. Otherwise, the deal could fail.
- **Too many eggs in one basket:** Too much concentration of revenue of the company being provided by one or a small number of customers can be fatal for a company and may render it unsalable or unlikely to succeed for long.

## Remember the cases illustrating the essentials:

- **Verify your objectives.** The seller had not fully evaluated the objectives and terminated a fully negotiated transaction at the final stage.
- **Unreasonable expectations.** The seller had a debt load that required unreasonable expectations of sale price to meet the seller's objectives. The delay and difficulty of the process led to a complete loss of the company.
- **Nothing to sell.** The seller ignored all of the features that a buyer requires, allowed her company to lose all value, and ended up with nothing to sell.
- **Unreported income and misrepresentation.** The seller was not honest with the buyer and lost at every turn of events due to misrepresentation.
- **Don't believe everything you hear.** A misleading broker bamboozled the seller into an egregious contract on a claim that was too good to be true.
- **Misleading intentions.** The buyer misled the seller, either intentionally or unintentionally, and the seller agreed to

finance the deal with an earn-out that was too good to be true.

- **Obstinate posturing.** The seller ignored possible solutions to his objectives, waiting for a deal that was too good to be true.
- **Lack of customer retention can be tragic.** The sellers were unable to assure or assist in the retention of the customer base. The sale nearly failed, and then the company nearly went under. The sale agreement required renegotiation twice in order to bring the price in line with the earnings and to salvage the transaction.

# APPENDIXES

## I. Type of Sale and Taxation Considerations

The type of legal entity and the tax considerations are discussed here. They were not discussed in detail under the negotiations sections, as they would require legal and financial professionals to determine the correct structures that best serve the buyer and the seller.

## II. Unusual Cases that Illustrate Special Situations in Business Valuation and Sales

- unsupported pricing
- a case for liquidation
- an usual business

## Appendix I: Type of Sale and Taxation Considerations

**Type of sale:** The type of sale is important for both parties as well. Most small business sales are asset sales, whereby the assets included in the sale are furniture, fixtures, equipment, inventory, goodwill, intangible assets, and sometimes accounts receivable. Not included in an asset sale usually are cash, cash equivalents, and all liabilities. Sometimes, equipment financing or lease agreements are assigned to the buyer. Typically, the seller keeps cash and cash equivalents and pays all creditors. The buyer would then need to provide working capital for daily operations as accounts receivable builds up in order to sustain the normal cash flow of the business. Larger businesses are normally stock sales, whereby the buyer acquires the outstanding shares of stock in the corporation and retains all assets and liabilities of the corporation. In this event, there would generally be a noncompetition agreement from the principals of the corporation and perhaps an employment contract for some of the principals.

**Taxation considerations:** The type of sale is important for both parties due to tax considerations. These are some suggestions of taxation issues that should be discussed and confirmed with your accountant for your specific case:

- Purchase of stock normally cannot be depreciated.
- Some assets can usually be depreciated.
- Sale of stock is usually only taxable if there is a capital gain and then at capital gain rates.
- Asset sales can sometimes incur a recapture of depreciation taken by seller in prior years, which may not be advantageous for the seller.
- If the sale of the business is a stock sale, the corporation remains in place, and only the ownership of the stock changes.
- If the sale is an asset sale, the structure of the sale can affect both the buyer and seller. Future taxation can affect the buyer; taxation of the sale proceeds can affect the seller.
- Taxation is generally based on the gain made on the sale, whether it is stock in the company or sale of the assets. The gain would be the difference between the sale price of the

assets or stock and the amount (or basis) of the initial cost remaining on the books after prior depreciation.

- Taxes on the sale of assets in the sale of a business or the sale of stock are normally calculated at the capital gain rate, which is sometimes at a lower rate than ordinary income.
- Taxation usually occurs in the year when the seller receives the money.
- If the sale structure includes assets allocated to a training or employment contract, noncompetition agreement, or similar assets, these may be taxed as ordinary income rather than as capital gains.
- If a portion of the assets is allocated to furniture, machinery, and equipment that have been depreciated partially or fully, there may be a recapture of depreciation required of the seller if the allocation of such assets is greater than the adjusted basis of the asset on the books of the seller.
- If a portion of the assets is allocated to goodwill, the buyer may depreciate that portion, perhaps over a fifteen-year rather than a longer period, which could be a tax advantage for the buyer.
- The buyer may deduct any portions of the assets allocated to training contracts or future employment as ordinary expenses as they are paid, which may be a tax advantage for the buyer.
- If the sale contract includes an installment sale, the seller would be taxed only for gain on the portion of the sale price received, as it is received. This could be a tax advantage for the seller.

These summaries of taxation effects are not completely defined and abbreviated for simplicity and merely indicate the impact of taxation considerations in the negotiation process. Your accountant and/or tax attorney should be involved in this process so the taxation issues specific to the case at hand are properly considered and factored into the perceived proceeds of the sale.

## Allocation of Assets

A sale of assets must include an allocation of the purchase price into certain asset classes, which include:

- **Class I:** Cash and cash equivalents
- **Class II:** Securities
- **Class III:** Accounts receivable
- **Class IV:** Inventory
- **Class V:** Machinery, equipment, real estate
- **Class VI:** Intangible assets except goodwill
- **Class VII:** Goodwill

The Internal Revenue Service requires this allocation, and it must be reported on Internal Revenue Code Form 8594.

## Legal Forms of Business Entities

Some businesses are formed as sole proprietorships, some as partnerships, some as C corporations, and some as subchapter S corporations. The structure of the business might have a direct effect on the taxation considerations.

If the business is a C corporation and the assets are sold but not the corporate entity, it will be a sale of assets by the corporation. All proceeds would normally remain in the corporation and be taxed accordingly. Any proceeds then being distributed to the shareholders could be taxed upon the shareholders individually. If a business is an S corporation and the corporation sells the assets, the proceeds would normally pass through to the shareholders and be taxed individually.

A typical business transfer agreement provides the agreed terms for all of the essential matters for the buyer and seller. All issues should be agreed upon before an offer is accepted and sent to escrow or a closing attorney.

# Appendix II

## Unusual Cases

### Case History: Unsupported Pricing

> The owner of a company in the business of film stock footage engaged me as a business advisor to assist him in selling his company. The company owned thousands of reels of film clips that had been accumulated over several decades. These clips were from discarded cuts of movies, newsreels, and numerous other sources. They covered virtually every conceivable subject matter. Two libraries had been acquired from former owners. The business of stock footage involved selling scenes or clips of various subjects and periods of time to film producers to assist them in completing a time sequence or an action scene of sorts and to avoid the cost of re-creating the scene.
>
> The disorganized owner of the company failed to provide any financial information for a basis of a valuation. He

had lingering debts and was without finances to promote the business. In spite of this, the collection appeared to have intrinsic value for a film industry buyer. The owner thought the collection should be worth a million dollars or more. I suggested that, due to the lack of any support for a value and the limited market for such an asset, an asking price of $250,000 would have a better chance of attracting attention and a higher price would be a deterrent to interest.

The collection was offered for sale for $250,000. Interest was attracted from around the United States and Europe. Numerous interested parties were communicated with over a period of several months. A showroom was created at a major film studio in Hollywood for display of the collection and showing of interesting film clips from the collection to attract interest.

As the marketing plan continued and all parties became more familiar with the stock footage industry, it became clear that the biggest obstacle to marketing this type of collection was the lack of digitization, that is, conversion from film to digital format. The bigger stock footage companies had gone to digitization, which made distribution and use of film clips much easier and practical. The cost of digitization at that time was very expensive, which was not possible for the collection owner. This limited the market for the collection and reduced the value considerably.

> The owner of these stock footage libraries had, in the meantime, borrowed money from individuals using these assets as collateral. Eventually, upon the debts becoming seriously delinquent, the court ordered me to sell the collection to satisfy the outstanding debts. The collection was eventually sold to a Chicago stock footage company for $40,000, after negotiation of the only offer that was solicited.
>
> I was able to retain, for the benefit of the owner, a collection of public domain news clips from a major news organization, which contained reels of clips for every year from 1929 through 1970. The owner was delighted to have salvaged anything from such a disorganized and sloppily run business.

This is a case of unsupported pricing. It was an unusual case due to the uniqueness of the business, the limited industry, and the lack of information available initially about the industry. Although the collection had rare and unique film clips, a buyer's knowledge of the content and the potential income to be derived was too subjective and uncertain, and the cost of making the material marketable caused a reduction of value and was a big obstacle to a sale.

## Case History: A Case for Liquidation

> I was asked to provide counsel for a gentleman in determining an exit plan for his company. This company did precision grinding for close tolerance metal parts, primarily for the aircraft industry. They had been in

business for many years and had enjoyed a viable business, which had declined over a period of several years. He owned his building, an attractive industrial structure with modern offices in an industrial center in a metropolitan area.

The profit and loss statements for the previous two years were as follows:

| PRECISION GRINDING COMPANY<br>P&L Comparisons<br>2001–2002 | | |
|---|---|---|
| | 2001 | 2002 |
| **Sales** | 529,700 | 433,356 |
| Cost of goods sold | 299,415 | 240,733 |
| **Gross Profit** | 230,285 | 192,623 |

The above section indicates a healthy profit margin but very limited gross revenue for a manufacturing company. It also reflects a decline in sales of almost 20 percent over the previous year.

| **Expenses** | | | | |
|---|---|---|---|---|
| | Auto | | 7,960 | 11,639 |
| | Depreciation | | 1,699 | 1,479 |
| | Dues and subscriptions | | 287 | 504 |
| | Equipment rental | | 42,788 | 36,000 |
| | Insurance-General | | 6,085 | 10,546 |
| | Insurance-Health | | 25,755 | 28,622 |
| | Interest | | 3,168 | |
| | Laundry | | 3,169 | 1,846 |
| | Legal and professional | | 10,929 | 4,970 |
| | Payroll services | | 2,182 | 1,926 |
| | Pension plan costs | | 4,702 | 5,716 |
| | Postage | | 309 | 692 |

| | | | | |
|---|---|---|---|---|
| | Promotion | | 2,941 | 2,513 |
| | Rent | | 39,000 | 33,000 |
| | Repairs and maintenance | | 10,402 | 9,411 |
| | Salaries-Officers | | 20,000 | |
| | Salaries and wages | | 33,344 | 27,327 |
| | Taxes and licenses | | 27,816 | 15,390 |
| | Telephone | | 4,006 | 4,660 |
| | Travel | | 408 | 438 |
| | Utilities | | 17,288 | 17,853 |
| **Total Expenses** | | | 264,240 | 214,532 |
| **Other Income** | | | 1,148 | 330 |
| **Net Income before Taxes** | | | (32,807) | (21,579) |

The owner's income was primarily received from rent for the premises, which he owned personally, and rent for some of the equipment that he owned personally. The above section indicates that the owner was not well paid, and in the second year, he received less rent for the premises and equipment and no salary. After all operating expenses were deducted, there was no net income in either year. There simply was insufficient revenue to cover basic operating expenses.

| | | | | |
|---|---|---|---|---|
| **Adjustments** | | | | |
| | Owner compensation | | 20,000 | |
| | Owner payroll taxes | | 1,600 | |
| | Depreciation | | 1,699 | 1,479 |
| | Interest | | 3,168 | |
| | Interest and dividends | | (1,148) | (330) |
| | Eqpt rent paid to owner | | 41,788 | 36,000 |
| **Total Adjustments** | | | 67,107 | 37,149 |
| **Discretionary Earnings** | | | 34,300 | 15,570 |

After adjustments to reflect discretionary earnings, the picture was clear: sales would have to increase substantially in order to provide enough gross profit to cover operating expenses and a reasonable income for the owner.

After considering this, the owner felt that increasing sales was not possible in the current market for their area of expertise. Their sources of business in previous years had come from major aircraft parts manufacturers as well as smaller makers. The demand for aircraft parts in the area had declined, and an increase in the next few years did not appear to be likely. The equipment owned by the company and the owner had significant value on the used equipment market. The building they occupied, which the company owner owned, had good value on a rental basis or in an orderly sale of the property. The owner was retirement age and had no employee or family member capable of running the company. The decision was made to liquidate.

This was a good case for liquidation. It actually worked out well for the owner and was the only realistic disposition of the company.

## Case History: Film Production Prop Rental

This example is a company that rented props to the movie industry.

> Two people operated this company on a part-time basis in the production sets business. They created sets for a movie production company. Over a period of years, they accumulated a warehouse full of various furnishings, clothing, and artifacts that were useful for production companies in building sets. They had limited business records to support income. They had one full-time person who maintained the store/warehouse and checked items in and out. This is an unusual type of business, and in lieu of any substantial financial records, it was suggested that the real value of the company was the inventory. Although it was difficult to determine, the parties met over several

> days inspecting and noting the entire inventory and finally agreed upon an inventory value of $233,000. This became the purchase price.
>
> The buyer paid the seller $30,000 down, with payments of $10,000 due in thirty days and $10,000 due in sixty days. The balance was then payable with interest at $5,185 per month until paid in full. The sellers were able to support the prior sales at a level that would justify the payment terms. The sellers had a security agreement on the inventory as collateral, which was filed with the state until the note was paid in full.

This is a case of an extremely limited buyer market and an unusual business. There were no historical financials to support an income stream, so the company actually merely sold the inventory, which was valued greater than the income would have supported.

The seller had collateral, which would be accessible for inspection and foreclosure in the event the note was not paid as agreed. It was the type of business that would tolerate inefficient management because, in many cases, it was the only place that a particular item could be acquired. This made the large seller note acceptable for the seller.

# Glossary of Financial Terms Used in This Publication

**accounts receivable:** Amounts owed to company by customers for goods sold or services rendered

**accounts payable:** Amounts owed to suppliers by company for goods or services purchased

**acquisition:** Purchasing or buying; acquiring a business

**amortization:** Deduction as an expense of a portion of the cost of certain intangible costs over a specified period of time, such as organizational expenses, patents, and copyrights

**asset:** Any tangible item owned by company, such as furniture, fixtures, equipment; any intangible item owned by the company, such as patents and copyrights

**balance sheet:** A financial statement that lists all assets at cost, all liabilities at the balance owed, and the capital structure, including invested capital, stock sales, and retained earnings

**cash flow:** Net income of the business plus noncash expenses, such as depreciation and amortization

**cost of goods sold:** Purchased material, direct labor, and other items directly required to provide goods or services sold

**current ratio:** A ratio calculated by dividing the current assets by the current liabilities to determine the liquidity of a company

**depreciation:** Deduction as an expense of a portion of the cost of assets of the company as the asset loses value

**discretionary earnings:** Earnings of the company plus owner benefits, perquisites, and non-business-related expenses paid by the company

**divestitures:** The sale or other disposition of a company or portion thereof

**earnings:** Profits of the company as expressed in various forms, such as EBT, EAT, EBITDA, and discretionary earnings

**EAT:** Earnings after taxes

**EBIT:** Earnings before interest and taxes

**EBITDA:** Earnings before interest, taxes, depreciation, and amortization

**EBITDA+OC:** EBITDA plus owner's compensation

**goodwill:** A value placed on the reputation of the company, owner relationships, and operational techniques that enhance the value of the company; a portion of the sale price not considered tangible assets

**gross profit:** Total sales of the business less the direct costs of goods sold, not including operating expenses

**intangible assets:** Assets other than furniture, fixtures, and equipment, such as patents, copyrights, goodwill, trade secrets, franchises, and distribution rights

**inventory:** All goods provided for sale by a company either as raw material, works in progress, or finished goods

**mergers:** Joining two or more companies to operate as one

**operating expenses:** General and administrative expenses not directly allocated to merchandise or services sold to customers, such as rent, office expenses, insurance, payroll, telephone, utilities, and so forth

**net profit:** Profit of the company after deducting cost of goods and operating expenses

**PEG:** Private equity group; an investment group that acquires businesses

**perquisites:** Benefits received by the owner other than monetary remuneration

**risk premium:** An adjustment to value based on the risk of loss of, a return on, or a return of the investment or any portion thereof

**tangible assets:** Furniture, fixtures, equipment, or tools; sometimes referred to as fixed assets

**working capital:** Capital required to finance normal operations, such as cash on hand and accounts receivable

# Index